OLYMPIC TRACK AND FIELD TECHNIQUES

An Illustrated Guide to Developing Champions

OLYMPIC TRACK AND FIELD TECHNIQUES
An Illustrated Guide
to Developing Champions

Tom Ecker, Fred Wilt, and Jim Hay

PARKER PUBLISHING COMPANY, INC. West Nyack, N.Y.

Library of Congress Cataloging in Publication Data

Ecker, Tom.
  Olympic track and field techniques.

  1. Track-athletics. 2. Olympic Games, Munich, 1972.
I. Wilt, Fred, joint author. II. Hay,
James G., joint author. III. Title.
GV1060.5.E285   796.4'2   74-1034
ISBN 0-13-633990-5

Other Books by the Authors

Championship Track and Field
By Tom Ecker (Prentice-Hall, Inc.)

Championship Football
By Tom Ecker with Paul Jones (Prentice-Hall, Inc.)

Pista y Campo de Campeonato
by Tom Ecker (Editorial Diana, Mexico)

Track and Field Dynamics
by Tom Ecker (Tafnews Press, Inc.)

Illustrated Guide to Olympic Track and Field Techniques
by Tom Ecker and Fred Wilt (Parker Publishing Company, Inc.)

International Track and Field Coaching Encyclopedia
by Fred Wilt and Tom Ecker (Parker Publishing Company, Inc.)

How They Train
by Fred Wilt (Tafnews Press, Inc.)

Run-Run-Run
by Fred Wilt (Tafnews Press, Inc.)

The Jumps: Contemporary Theory, Technique and Training
by Fred Wilt (Tafnews Press, Inc.)

Motivation and Coaching Psychology
by Fred Wilt and Ken Bosen (Tafnews Press, Inc.)

The Biomechanics of Sports Techniques
by Jim Hay (Prentice-Hall, Inc.)

FOREWORD

In the Olympic year of 1972 a remarkable improvement in track and field performances was noted. At the Olympic Games of Munich many national, continental and world records were bettered by competitors coming from all parts of the world. Great performances, once considered to be the limits of human potential, are today achieved by juniors and sometimes unknown average-class competitors.

There are many reasons for the continuous improvement in performances. Track and field is gaining increasingly greater popularity, larger numbers of young people are coming in contact with systematic coaching, and greater and better selection is possible. Technical developments help in achieving better performances. Modern coaching methods are improved by the application of the results of research in all the related sciences.

A competitor, however, will only be able to reach his potential if he has a good knowledge of the technique of his event on which to form his own personal style. The personal style depends on the individual's abilities—body structure, speed, strength, endurance, muscular coordination, sense of balance and rhythm. Top performances are the result of the application of the right technique expressed in personal style.

The study of the correct movements of great athletes and the perfection of their techniques contributes greatly to fast and correct learning of the technique most suitable to the individual.

The authors, Tom Ecker, Fred Wilt and Jim Hay, distinguished experts in track and field, present in this book the technique and style of the Olympic champions of Munich with technical analyses by world-renowned coaches, specialists in their events. It is an excellent work, useful for coaches and competitors as well as for athletic fans. The authors have made a great effort and every page reflects their love of track and field athletics. I hope readers will study this interesting and most instructive book with the same devotion that the authors have shown in compiling it.

I take this opportunity to express my heartiest congratulations to the authors, Tom Ecker, Fred Wilt and Jim Hay, and to all those who have cooperated with them. I warmly recommend this book to all those who have an interest in learning or teaching perfect techniques in the track and field events.

Otto Szymiczek

President,
International Track & Field
Coaches Association

PREFACE

Sports Technique Analysis has grown from a rather undisciplined art form into a complicated science during the past two decades. While the leading coaches once relied on simple descriptions of techniques, their present-day counterparts strive not merely to describe what they see, but to account for it in scientific terms.

The use of motion picture loop films (a technique developed by one of the contributors to this book, Britain's Geoffrey Dyson), sequence photographs, and computers have made it possible to analyze techniques to a degree not even contemplated 20 years ago.

But the improvements of sports techniques through analysis requires more than just the ability to analyze; there must also be outstanding sports performances to emulate, and excellent photographs of those performances to study. In this book, OLYMPIC TRACK AND FIELD TECHNIQUES, we have the best of all three worlds—the *best photographs* of the *best athletes*, analyzed by the *best of the world's track and field experts*.

Pictured are the championship techniques of world-class athletes who have won 30 Olympic gold medals, setting eight world and 19 Olympic records in the process.

The 25 contributing coaches represent 14 different nations, six continents, and literally hundreds of years of successful coaching experience. They are the best in the field.

The photographs were taken at the Olympic Games by the IAAF's official Olympic photographer, Toni Nett of Germany, and by other top professional photographers.

11

Collecting track and field information has long been a hobby of the three editors of this book. We attend coaching clinics—both in the USA and abroad—sometimes as speakers, but more often as listeners. We correspond with coaches from all parts of the world. We read as many track and field books and articles as we can locate; we write as many track and field nooks and articles as time permits. Our long range goal is to continue to gather, organize, and disseminate as many new ideas as time ans energy will allow. This book is part of that process.

Tom Ecker
Fred Wilt
Jim Hay

CONTENTS

13

OLYMPIC TRACK AND FIELD TECHNIQUES

An Illustrated Guide to Developing Champions

PART ONE

The Running Events

1

FUNDAMENTAL MECHANICS OF RUNNING AND HURDLING

Author: **Fred Wilt**—competitor, coach, author, lecturer—has won international acclaim in the world of track and field. As an athlete he won eleven national distance championships, set one world record, competed in two Olympics, and won the coveted Sullivan Award. Now he devotes most of his spare time to the furthering of man's track and field knowledge—collecting information, writing books and articles, editing *Track Technique* magazine, delivering clinic lectures, and coaching young runners.

Even though Sir Isaac Newton (1642-1727) first clearly enunciated the three laws of motion upon which classical Newtonian mechanics is based, not until fairly recently have these laws been applied to human running in an effort to find answers to questions concerning such things as optimum lean, stride length, arm and leg action, and foot placement.

Human running is extremely complex when analyzed in its complete mechanical detail. Nevertheless, through a superficial application of mechanical principles, it is possible to provide information of genuine practical value in terms of technique and form.

It is common knowledge that no two humans have the same fingerprints. By the same token, each athlete differs from every other to at least some slight extent in muscle origins and insertions, size and length of muscles, bone structure, posture, flexibility, height, weight, personality, and various other features that influence form and technique in running. Because of individual physical makeup, form is strictly an individual proposition, and good form may be described only in general terms. Accordingly, it is a grave error for one runner to blindly copy any aspect of the form of another.

In order to describe running, it is first useful to recognize that racewalking may be superficially described as progression by steps so taken that unbroken contact with the ground is maintained—the heel of the advancing foot contacting the ground before the toe of the rear foot leaves the ground. Walking involves pushing the body forward and out of balance, while it is supported over one leg, and then bringing the swinging, rear leg forward in time to prevent the body from falling. Speed in walking is limited by the step-length—determined by the possible distance between the feet while both are in contact with the ground—and by the time necessary for the rear leg to swing forward to prevent the body from falling with each step.

Human running is a form of locomotion devoid of any theoretical limit on speed on such mechanical grounds as found in walking. Speed is increased in running by causing the body to "float" in the air with both feet off the ground for a short time with each step. During this time the step is made longer than the span of the legs would otherwise permit. In running, there is never a phase of "double support," when both feet are on the ground simultaneously. The rear leg always starts swinging forward before the front foot contacts the ground. Contrary to walking, there is always a period of "double float" in each running step when both feet are off the ground.

The action of each leg may be arbitrarily divided into three phases, regardless of the running speed:

1. The supporting phase. This begins the instant the foot contacts the ground about 12 inches (30 cm.) ahead of a point directly below the body's center of gravity (CG)—Figure 1. It is the shortest of the three phases, and ends when the body's CG has moved ahead of the foot in contact with the ground (Figure 2). The faster the running speed, the closer the foot approaches to grounding directly beneath the body's CG.

Figure 1   **Figure 2**

2. Driving phase. Immediately upon completion of the supporting phase, the driving phase begins and continues until the foot leaves the ground well behind the CG (Figure 3). Throughout this phase the body is propelled forward by extension of levers at the hip, knee, ankle, and toes in that order, acting behind the body's CG is a pushing action. Increased stride length must always result from greater force being exerted by the leg acting behind the body's CG in the driving phase, rather than stretching the leading leg grotesquely forward in the recovery phase, and attempting to ground the foot farther ahead of the body's CG in a futile effort to "claw" the body forward. The runner should have a feeling of pushing the ground away from behind throughout the driving phase.

3. The recovery phase. This starts when the toe of the foot in the driving phase leaves the ground behind the body's CG, and ends when the same foot is again planted slightly ahead of the CG to start another supporting phase.

Body lean in running is a function of acceleration—the greater the

Figure 3

acceleration, the greater the body lean. At uniform speed, the body is nearly erect (i.e. no acceleration, no lean). Forward body lean is always greater at the start because it is here that acceleration is greatest. Running into a strong headwind would, of course, require some adjustment in forward body lean, even at uniform speed. The most accurate appraisal of a runner's true body lean may be seen when the knees are closest together (Figure 4), while an illusion of forward lean may be observed when viewing the runner from the side at the end of the driving phase when the leg is extended behind the body (Figure 5).

Stride frequency (cadence) among middle-distance runners is usually around 3½ strides per second. In sprinting, it is around 4½ and occasionally (for brief periods) as much as 5 strides per second.

Stride length at middle-distance speeds varies from 5 to 6 feet (1.5-1.8 m.) while in sprinting it ranges generally between 7 and 8½ feet (2.1-2.6 m.). As a general rule, it may be said that stride length is a function of running speed. The slower the speed, the shorter the stride and the faster the speed, the longer the runner's stride. Thus the stride is shortest in jogging and longest in sprinting.

Figure 4   **Figure 5**

Both understriding and overstriding are faults. Each runner has his own personal optimum stride length for any given running speed, depending upon leg length, joint flexibility, and numerous other factors.

It requires 43-45 strides to spring 100 yards, and 47-49 strides to sprint 100 meters. About 1,000 strides are required to run a mile. Top recorded sprinting speed is 36 feet per second (11 m./sec).

Running speed = candence × stride length. Since maximum cadence among humans seems limited (4½-5 strides per second), the greatest potential for increasing speed is increasing stride length resulting from the exertion of greater force in the driving phase of the stride.

As a runner moves faster and faster, there is less and less time in which to exert force behind the CG during the driving phase of the stride. Thus as running speed increases, the potential for impulse (force × time) is reduced. It is here that we find one great difference between top-class sprinters and those who possess less sprinting speed. The great sprinter can still exert force behind the CG in the driving phase of the stride, even though the time becomes progressively shorter in which to exert such force. Another feature which may differentiate the great sprinter is his ability to accelerate the leg forward in the recovery phase, which by reaction increases the force exerted by the driving leg.

The height to which the knee is lifted in front of the body during the recovery phase is dependent upon the running speed. The faster the running speed, the higher the knee is lifted in front. The limit of the forward swing of the recovery knee coincides with the completion of the driving phase of the opposite leg.

In all running, including sprinting, at the conclusion of the recovery phase the leading foot sweeps downward, and apparently backward, to initiate the supporting phase of the stride. The outer border of the ball of the foot first contacts the track as the supporting phase of the stride begins. The faster the running speed the more forward (toward the toes) is the point on the outer border of the foot where contact is first made with the ground. Immediately after this first contact, the heel of the foot comes naturally to the ground. No effort should be made to prevent this. As the heel touches the ground without inhibition, the foot rolls inward, toward the midline of the body. As the body rides forward, over, and beyond the foot which is momentarily flat on the ground, the heel lifts and ground contact is broken with the inside edge of the ball-toe of the foot, to conclude the driving phase of the stride.

It is sometimes argued that running, especially sprinting, is faster if the heels do not touch the ground. This is quite definitely wrong. Work = force × distance. If the distance over which force may be exerted is reduced by failure to permit the heel to touch the ground with each stride, then the range over which work may be accomplished is significantly shortened, and the potential for speed is obviously reduced.

Ideally, the inner border of each foot should touch the ground along a straight line during the supporting and driving phases. The feet should not be placed wide apart laterally, or one in front of the other in a straight line, as both positions cause an inefficient, side-to-side motion when running.

The line of force of the leg through the hip in the driving phase of the stride is offset from the body's CG. Thus, an off-center or "eccentric" thrust of the left leg acting through the left hip, during the driving phase, coupled with the forward lifting of the right leg in the recovery phase of this (right) leg, causes the hips to rotate counterclockwise in a horizontal plane (when viewed from above). The body is lifted simultaneously no more than necessary to counteract the pull of gravity as the runner is projected forward. For every action, there must be an equal and opposite reaction. The reaction to the forward projection of the body is absorbed by the ground. The reaction to the twisting actions caused by the eccentric thrust of the left leg are absorbed by the upper body. In this instance, as the hips move counterclockwise in a horizontal plane, the upper body (arms, trunk, and shoulders) move clockwise in a parallel horizontal plane.

During the running stride the upper body moves either clockwise or counterclockwise in a horizontal plane, in reaction to the hips moving in the opposite direction in a parallel plane. The obvious result is that the right arm and shoulder move forward and backward in coordination with the left leg, while the left arm and shoulder move backward and forward in coordination with the right leg.

Because the cadence is less in middle- and long-distance running, there is sufficient time to allow the trunk and shoulders to absorb much of the reaction to the twisting movements created by the eccentric thrust of the legs. This permits an energy-conserving use of somewhat mild arm action and flowing shoulder-twist as seen in middle- and long-distance running.

In sprinting the cadence is so fast the shoulders cannot twist and untwist quickly enough to absorb the reaction to the frequent and powerful eccentric leg thrusts during the driving phase. For this reason, the sprinter seeks to keep his shoulders steady and absorb the reaction to the eccentric thrust of the legs by forceful and faster (though more tiring) arm action over a wide range. This range of arm motion in sprinting is approximately the same in front and behind the shoulder axis.

The upper arms move relatively straight backward and forward. The lower arms move "around" the trunk in a slight cross-body direction in front, especially in middle- and long-distance running, but do not cross an imaginary vertical plane bisecting the body into right and left halves. In sprinting the lower arms tend to move more directly backward and forward with less cross-body action than seen in running at slower speeds, and the hands swing as high as eye level in front and no more than about a foot behind the hipline.

During the forward swing of each arm, the elbow tends to remain bent at an angle of approximately 90 degrees, permitting it to move forward more rapidly due to a reduced moment of inertia (mass × radius squared) about its axis at the shoulder. This bend increases somewhat as the hands swing in front of the body.

As the arm moves backward during the driving phase of the leg on the opposite side of the body, the angle at the elbow increases (straightens) to the maximum extent at a point when the knees are closest together. As the arm continues backward, passing the hip, it again starts bending at the elbow. As it approaches the end of its path backward, it is again bent to a near 90 degree angle at the elbow, thus increasing its speed of motion to coincide with the final thrust of the leg on the opposite side of the body at the conclusion of the driving phase.

The hands are carried in a relaxed "cupped" position in both sprinting and running at slower speeds, as seen in the accompanying photos.

The arms "follow" the legs and absorb reaction to the eccentric thrust of the legs during the driving phase. Because action and reaction are interchangeable, a fast and powerful arm action may be used in sprinting to speed up the action of the legs.

The head should be aligned naturally with the trunk, and the eyes focused a few yards ahead. It may sometimes move somewhat from side to side in middle-distance running without upsetting body balance, and occupy a role in absorbing the reaction to the action of the eccentric leg-thrust during the driving phase of the stride. It is a mistake to throw back the head at the finish, as this tends to shorten the stride and straighten the trunk.

The essential and involuntary process of breathing should be subjected to the least possible resistance and interference. For this reason, the runner should inhale and exhale through both the mouth and nose.

Athletes who run naturally always find their best and most economical form or style by much training at a variety of speeds over various distances and surfaces. It is therefore unnecessary to "teach" an athlete to run correctly. Difficulty in running form is encountered only when the athlete departs from his natural style and attempts to use some artificially imposed motion, such as overstriding or toe-running.

Sprinting is running at the maximum speed of which an athlete is capable. Anything less than top speed is not sprinting. The form of any one athlete when sprinting will differ in terms of intensity from his form when running at slower speeds. In sprinting the cadence is faster, the stride is longer, the heel of the recovery foot rises higher toward the hip, the knee of the recovery leg rises higher in front, there is less shoulder motion, the arm action is more vigorous, and there is a considerably greater fatiguing effect than when running at lesser speeds.

The start in sprint and hurdles races is accomplished most efficiently with a "medium" starting block spacing. This places the front block 15-18 inches (38-46 cm.) behind the starting line, with a space of 16-20 inches (40-50 cm.) between the blocks. In the "set" position the front knee is bent at an angle of about 90 degrees, the hips are slightly higher than the shoulders, the rear knee is bent at an angle of slightly greater than 90 degrees, the body's weight is supported equally between the hands and front foot, the head is held in natural alignment with the body, and the eyes are focused somewhere between the starting line and 2-3 feet (60-90 cm.) beyond this line. High hurdlers using an eight-stride approach to the first barrier place the take-off foot on the front block and the lead foot on the rear block. The feet are reversed for the seldom seen seven-stride approach.

Hurdling is sprinting over obstacles. The problem is to clear the barriers in such a way as to interfere least with the athlete's sheer sprinting speed. Thus, hurdling technique is a modification of sprinting form. Because of the exact height and distance between barriers as specified by the rules, and the anatomical limitations imposed upon human locomotion, the possibilities for improving hurdle times are concerned mainly with stride cadence and hurdle clearance, rather than increased stride length.

In the 120 yards (110 cm.) hurdles event, the sum of eight strides to the first 42-inch (107 cm.) hurdle, nine times three strides between hurdles (total 27), and five finishing strides is 40. This sum added to the ten strides over the barriers makes a total of 50 strides in the race. For a 13.0 second 120 yards hurdles result, the average cadence is 50 strides divided by 13.0 seconds or 3.84 strides per second. When compared to maximum sprint cadence (4½-5 strides per second), it is obvious that one avenue for improvement in high hurdling is increased stride cadence.

To increase stride cadence without altering stride length requires drills involving (a) running specific short distances at faster cadence while using an extra stride length similar to the hurdler's average stride length between barriers, (b) being towed by a vehicle over short distances at a cadence much faster than would otherwise be possible, (c) treadmill running requiring maximum possible cadence, and (d) sprinting short distances over slightly downhill terrain using maximum cadence.

Skilled hurdlers sprint the 120 yards high hurdle event in a time only 2 seconds (or slightly less) slower than their time for sprinting an equal distance without barriers. The average time required to negotiate a hurdle is therefore only 0.2 second or slightly less. Thus hurdles clearance technique should strive to interfere least with normal sprinting action. In achieving such an objective, the hurdler's limbs are displaced in such a way as to avoid contact with the barriers, while landing beyond the hurdle in positions to return immediately to normal sprinting action.

Each of the usual eight strides to the first hurdle in high hurdling is longer than the preceding stride, except the final step. Any adjustment in the approach should occur in the fourth, fifth, and sixth strides. The final approach stride is 2-4 inches shorter than the penultimate stride. The purpose of shortening this last step is to rotate the trunk forward so the drive from the take-off foot will project the body with an almost horizontal lean or "body-dip" across the hurdle. This lean must be initiated while the body is still in contact with the ground, as the flight-path of the hurdler's CG while airborne follows a predetermined parabolic path and cannot be altered in the air.

To clear the hurdle, the lead-leg at take off must be lifted fast, with knee well-bent (Figure 6). A high, fast pick-up of this knee encourages

Figure 6

continuation of general springing action, increases the force of thrust off the ground by the take-off leg, leaves behind the take-off leg (trail leg) and causes a desirable "splits" position between the legs after take off so the take-off leg may come forward late but fast, increases body-dip in reaction to the fast-rising knee-lift, and is much faster than when using a straight lead leg. The speed of lead leg lift determines the speed of hurdle clearance. As a practical matter, the hurdler should try to move the lead knee and foot so fast that the foot cannot be seen, thus producing a wide split between the legs at take off.

As the leading leg is lifted quickly for hurdle clearance at take off, the arm opposite the lead leg is thrust forcefully forward. Some athletes wrap the leading arm (i.e., the arm opposite the lead leg) somewhat across the body, but later straighten and thrust it forward. The arm on the same side as the lead leg remains bent at the elbow in normal sprinting position, in readiness to drive forward in coordination with the trail leg's forward motion for the first "getaway" stride after clearance. *Note:* A "double arm action"—having both arms forward—during the hurdle clearance is not ideal, since this deviates from arm position in normal sprinting.

After full extension of the take-off leg, the heel of this limb rises immediately to the buttock, folding the lower leg to the thigh preparatory to the knee being swung well out to the side, upward and forward to bring the thigh parallel to the ground.

The leading foot reaches its highest point 6-12 inches (15-30 cm.) before the barrier, and the athlete's CG reaches its zenith about 1 foot (30 cm.) in front of the hurdle. From this high point, the hurdler comes down across the obstacle during the clearance.

The near horizontal body-dip initiated at take off permits raising the seat and lowering the trunk in relation to the hurdler's CG while crossing the barrier with a minimum lifting of the CG. The lower the athlete's flight path over the hurdle, the more quickly he may regain ground contact and continue sprinting.

Before the athlete's seat reaches the barrier, the lead leg begins to straighten, cuts across the hurdle rail, and continues down toward the other side with heel of the foot leading this action (Figure 7).

Ideally, the head and shoulders should face forward at all times, with minimum deviation from their normal positions during sprinting. Dropping the head while over the obstacle may produce a flatter layout during clearance, although this advantage must be weighed against the disadvantage of a possible momentary interference with the athlete's vision.

When most of the body weight is beyond the barrier and the lead leg is well on its way to the ground, the trail leg passes over the hurdle with its foot "cocked" slightly upward to avoid striking the rail with the toes. The crotch reaches the barrier before the knee of the trail leg. As it passes "late but fast" over the hurdle rail, the trail leg is parallel to the ground and makes a right angle with the leading leg.

As it passes about about the hurdle rail, the knee of the trail leg is lifted up high toward and almost to the chest, to insure an optimum "getaway" stride of about 5 feet (152 cm.)—Figure 8.

Figure 7   **Figure 8**

The foot of the lead leg lands 3 feet 9 inches-4 feet 6 inches (114-137 cm.) beyond the hurdle after clearance. The landing point must be beneath and slightly behind the body's CG to insure immediate return to sprinting action. There is nothing to be gained by preventing the heel from touching the ground at this correct landing point. The extreme body dip over the hurdle decreases to the body-angle of normal sprint action (in accordance with acceleration) as the lead foot is grounded.

With the changes in the position of the legs as the hurdler pivots over the hurdle in the just described clearance action, the arms also change position. The leading arm swings back, somewhat bent at the elbow, with the hand carried low. It sweeps backward, outside the knee of the trailing leg, which is now moving forward. If the elbow is bent and the hand carried low, a wide novice "swimming action" of this arm may be avoided.

Hurdlers are sometimes instructed to snap the lead leg down as the hurdle clearance is made in an effort to more quickly regain ground contact. This actually has the effect of prematurely raising the trunk in reaction, although it may not be so obvious as the action of the lead leg because the moment of inertia of this leg about a horizontal axis passing through the body's CG is less than the moment of inertia of the trunk about the same axis. Nevertheless, such a premature raising of the trunk may cause the trail leg to drop, and result in the foot striking the hurdle rail as it is brought through for the first getaway stride. *Note:* Insufficient body-dip during hurdle clearance is usually the cause of striking the hurdle with the foot or ankle of the trail leg.

Rather than attempting to snap down the lead leg, the hurdler should lift the trail leg through high, bringing the limb through laterally until the knee is near the chest in front, causing the lead leg to move downward in reaction to the upward-forward lifting of the trail leg. The faster the trailing leg is pulled through forward-upward, the faster the lead leg will move toward the ground. This is not to suggest the trail leg should be "hurried" (causing a jump to avoid striking the barrier), nor that it should be delayed. Rather the legs must move continuously throughout hurdle clearance with no "posed" position at any time.

The key to proper stride length between hurdles is often directly related to the length of the first stride after the lead leg is grounded beyond the hurdle. This stride must be a hard-driving effort of about 5 feet (150 cm.). A short first stride is ordinarily caused by lack of trail leg lift.

Clearing the hurdle causes the athlete to rotate simultaneously in several planes while in the air. For the purpose of reference, think of three anatomical planes passing through the body's CG as the frontal (a vertical plane that divides the body into front and rear halves), sagittal (a vertical plane that divides the body into right and left halves), and horizontal (a plane parallel to the ground that divides the body into upper and lower halves). As the athlete leaves the ground for hurdle clearance, there is forward rotation in a sagittal plane. As the trail leg is lifted laterally forward-upward, the trunk rotates downward ("sidewise") in reaction toward this upward-moving limb in a frontal plane. As the trail leg continues forward, passing the hurdle rail and sweeps laterally forward-upward toward the front of the body, the trunk rotates toward this forward moving limb in a horizontal plane. As the lead leg sweeps downward toward the ground for landing, the trunk moves upward by reaction in a sagittal plane.

The adverse aspect of these rotations may be minimized by an appropriate body-dip at take off, causing a flat hurdle-clearance, thus resulting in the body presenting a greater moment of inertia in a horizontal plane about a vertical axis passing through the CG. This moment of inertia is increased by the forward extension of the arm opposite the lead leg during the clearance. Such an increased moment of inertia about the vertical axis will permit a less pronounced reaction to the action of the trail leg in a horizontal plane.

The technique of clearing 42-inch hurdles applies generally to clearance of the 30-inch (76 cm.) barriers, with certain modifications. Because the hurdler's CG is well above the low hurdle rail, there is no need for the exaggerated body-dip. Extreme body-dip in clearing the low hurdles would require unnecessarily executing the dip, and then raising the trunk following each clearance. The forward lean at low-hurdle clearance should be merely sufficient to maintain proper sprinting form. There is little rise in head height in clearance. It is not necessary to lift the trail knee to hip level in crossing the barrier. Thus the extreme hip flexibility of high hurdling is not absolutely necessary in clearing these barriers.

The technique of clearing the intermediate (36-inch or 91.4 cm.) hurdles is roughly halfway between that of high- and low-hurdle clearance techniques. The pivot over the hurdle rail is slower than in either of the others. Economy of effort receives more attention here. Less body-dip is required than in high hurdling. Because horizontal speed is slower, the stepping action over the 36-inch barriers is less violent. The trail leg is not lifted so high as in high-hurdling. A first stride of around 5 feet is required after hurdle clearance in this event, as in the case of both the 30-inch and 42-inch barriers.

The technique of high-hurdle clearance can be generally applied to the women's 100 m. hurdles event, since the height of the barrier is 33 inches (83.8 cm.), and female athletes are usually shorter in stature than male performers in the high-hurdles event.

Hurdling should be considered a sprint race over barriers. The action throughout should present as little interruption as possible to sprinting form. Although for the purpose of description and analysis it may be useful to separate hurdle clearance into various phases, it is in reality a continuous coordinated effort, and not a series of separate parts.

2

THE SPRINT START

Athlete: **Valeriy Borzov,** *U.S.S.R.*

Olympic Competition:
100m.	1972	1st	10.1
200m.	1972	1st	20.0

Author: **Arthur Eustace** is one of New Zealand's leading coaches. A former champion in the 100, 120, and 220 yard hurdles, he represented New Zealand in the 1950 Empire Games and Fiji in the 1954 Commonwealth Games. He has served as Coach and Manager of the Fiji national team, as I.A.A.F. Coach of Ceylon, and as Coach of the New Zealand team at the 1973 Pacific Conference Games.

The benefit of an efficient crouch start is seen, not within the first three strides, but at about the 40 meter mark. Great acceleration with a transition into smooth, balanced, full-stride sprinting action as soon as possible is the aim of the sprinter.

The pictures we are analyzing are of Valeriy Borzov in a 200 meter start. He knows that in lane 5 there can be only four or five full-blooded driving strides before the sprinting action is adjusted to the need to manage the bend. Furthermore, in this start faulty adjustment of the front block allowed it to tip backwards during the final thrust of the front leg. Thus lesson 1 from this analysis must be *check that your blocks are properly adjusted—even in the Olympics!*

Ignoring the possible effects these two circumstances may have had upon this start, let us examine the evidence in the pictures.

Figure 1 On the mark. This is a bunched or "bullet" position. The blocks are about 6 inches (15 cm.) apart; the front block about 25 inches (63 cm.) from the line. Though this gives a rather hunched looking position, the athlete looks relaxed and the position of the head suggests that all his concentration is on the starter's voice.

Because the blocks are set on the outside of the lane at an angle to allow as much of a straight run as possible before acceleration is disturbed by the need to run in a curve, the left hand fingers are about 1 inch (2.5 cm.) behind the line.

Figure 2 Set. We do not see Borzov rise into this position but movie films of his start show a steady, smooth lift of the hips.

Block position combined with high hip position gives an angle of about 90 degrees at the front knee, which is most effective in terms of the leverage applied by the extensors of the knee. This is important since the

Figure 1   Figure 2   Figure 3   Figure 4

front leg provides the greater impulse of the two. The angle of the hip of this leg is less efficient, detracting a little from the power of the hip extensors. The rear knee is open to about 110 degrees with a more advantageous angle at the hip.

The fingers are strongly bridged allowing the shoulders to be as far above the track as possible. Even allowing for camera angle, the forward lean over the shoulders is minimal so that there is less body weight on the arms than in most sprinters. When the angle of the trunk is considered, the head is down in a natural position, avoiding tension around the neck.

Figures 3-4 At the gun the hips immediately move forward. The shoulders rise, but for 10 inches (25 cm.) of lift there is 10 inches (25 cm.) of forward displacement so we may compliment the athlete on the extent to which this initial thrust is forward rather than upward. By Figure 4 tension is gone from the fingers and forearms. The head stays down in an excellent position. The high support of the blocks prevents the right heel from sinking as the power is applied and little of its effect is dissipated. The right foot is already leaving its block in Figure 4.

Figures 5-7 The impulse of the rear leg is short and no time is lost in whipping it forward. Notice that it is recovered slightly sideways, the musculature of the hip making it very difficult to pull this knee through straight under the chest. The arms are quickly into a bent position, the right one kept bent and nicely under control at the rearmost part of the drive. The left arm, rather than following an "uppercutting" action, has been lifted sideways which is unusual. The head is still with the face to the track and the trunk is only a little above a horizontal position, an indication of the forward drive which has been developed and the high rate of acceleration. The contribution of the left leg to this forward drive

Figure 5   Figure 6   Figure 7

Figure 8   **Figure 9**   **Figure 10**

can be fully appreciated by comparing its fully extended position in Figure 15 with the right leg position in Figure 4 at the end of its "thrust."

Figures 8-9 The right knee comes forward very well but note how quickly the left leg is moving. Compare Figure 9 with Figure 18 and Figure 10 with Figure 19 to see how much further up this rear leg is than at any other time in the race. As it hits the track the right foot is being driven backwards in relation to the body's center of gravity. Lie matchsticks through the right ankle and the navel in Figures 8, 9 and 10 to see what is happening.

This first stride is about 39 inches (100 cm.), from toe on the track to left block position, which would be fine if the second stride was at least as long.

Figure 14   **Figure 15**   **Figure 16**

Figure 11   **Figure 12**   **Figure 13**

Figures 10-12 These pictures show fast recovery of the left leg; the knee coming through high under the chest produces a satisfying picture of power and vigor in Figure 11. The arms are being used vigorously to lead and balance the leg action. But this stride is only about 34-35 inches (87-89 cm.), appreciably shorter than the first one and this is not a good thing (see summary). The head has been lifted a little but there is no strain evident around the neck.

Figures 13-19 As rate of acceleration diminishes so the shoulders rise in relation to the hips. The amount of body lean which has been lost shows up when you compare Figure 12 with Figure 16. Knee lift is excellent, combining with a full thrust of the left leg to produce a stride of about 45 inches (115 cm.). We observe that the arm action is uneven, the

Figure 17   **Figure 18**   **Figure 19**

right elbow remaining bent while the left one is almost straight in Figure 19. There is a relaxed look about the hands, arms, shoulders and neck.

Summary

I do not think Borzov would be happy with this start. The pictures show that he jumped from the blocks through a bullet style, which often produces a long first stride. Nevertheless, in this case I think stride 2 is a recovery stride.

The first right foot placement is wide in the lane, the first left foot almost touches the line on the near side and then the second right foot placement is right back in a good line. Though some weaving is inevitable in a powerful start, this example is exaggerated and suggests that Borzov was not completely on balance.

The arm action is uneven which might be understandable further around the bend but not in the first three strides.

Despite all this we must be realistic and comment that the excellent explosive power displayed by Borzov is the outstanding feature of his start. The shortcomings revealed by the merciless slow-motion camera are put into perspective if our man is 1 meter ahead at the 50 meter mark.

3

THE 200m. STRIDE

Athlete: **Renate Stecher,** *East Germany*

Olympic Competition:

100m.	1972	1st	11.1
200m.	1972	1st	22.4 (World Record)

Authors: **Paul Ward** is track coach at the University of Kentucky. A former all-around thrower and professional football player, he coached track and field at California Western University, San Diego; Portland State University; and the University of Wisconsin, Parkside.

      Roy Griak, track and cross-country coach at the University of Minnesota, was manager of the U.S. track and field team at the 1972 Olympic Games. Formerly a highly successful coach of high school track and cross-country teams, Griak moved to the University of Minnesota in 1963, where his athletes have won ten individual and three team conference titles.

Figure 1   **Figure 2**   **Figure 3**

Figures 1, 7 & 12 Midsupport
phase. Figure 1 shows the exact midsupport phase, while Figures 7 & 12
show the runner just past this phase. In this phase the sprinter is well-
balanced and her entire weight is supported on a completely flat foot. The
center of gravity appears to be directly over the supporting foot and there
is a slight lean forward by the trunk. The recovery leg is flexed at the knee
to permit a quick swing through in preparation for the maximum knee lift
at take off. The elbows are flexed approximately 90 degrees. Note the
very relaxed style of the athlete, particularly in Figure 1.

Figure 2 Transition to take off (driving phase). As the runner moves
forward over the take-off foot the supporting leg is flexed at the knee,
lowering the center of gravity, while the heel of the support foot breaks
contact with the track surface. The time of contact of the sprinter's heel is

Figure 7   **Figure 8**   **Figure 9**

Figure 4   **Figure 5**   **Figure 6**

very short compared to that of a distance runner. There is a slight lean forward by the trunk at this instant. The recovery leg is continuing its forward movement with the knee flexed considerably. The right arm remains flexed at the elbow and is swinging forward at the shoulder joint in opposition to the recovery leg. The hands remain relaxed. There is slight rotation developing in the upper body that offsets the rotation produced in the lower body by the recovery leg. Indeed, this rotation must remain minimal for sprinters. The force generated here and at take off determines the length of the stride. The average stride length of female international class sprinters at full pace ranges from approximately 6 feet 9 inches (2.06m.) to 7 feet 5 inches (2.26m.). The support phase in full pace sprinting is shorter than the duration of the flight phase.

Figures 3 & 8 At this moment the knee lift is at its maximum while

Figure 10   **Figure 11**   **Figure 12**

the knee joint itself is beginning to extend forward in preparation for touchdown. The emphasis at this point should be on a strong thigh and knee extension of the driving leg combined with a maximum knee lift of the recovery leg. The thigh and knee extension of the driving leg is evidenced here by the apparent contraction of the hip and knee extensors of the driving leg. The angle of the rear leg to the horizontal appears to be approximately 65-70 degrees. The rear knee extension is not maximal but appears to be between 160-180 degrees.

Figures 4 & 9 At this point the sprinter is well balanced with the arms and legs in maximal opposition. The swing leg knee is beginning to extend forward in preparation for touchdown. The runner appears to remain relaxed at this instant.

Figures 5 & 10 The lead knee is extended so that the foot is in position to contact the running surface. The recovery leg at this time begins to flex at the knee to facilitate its rapid swing forward. The best sprinters accelerate the lead foot backwards at this moment, which may assist in reducing the braking force at touchdown. The arms and, to a lesser degree, the trunk offset the rotation produced in the lower body.

Figures 6 & 11 It appears that contact with the running surface of the leading foot is made on the lateral aspect of the ball of the foot, but is quickly flattened (see Figure 1) for the midsupport phase. The heel touch is of short duration in full pace sprinting and is difficult to detect. The center of gravity seems to be slightly behind the point of contact of the foot. The braking force is partially countered by the movement backward with respect to the center of gravity, of the lead foot as it contacts the running surface. The arms are swinging in opposition with approximately a 90 degree flexion at the elbows.

Summary

The pictures show the runner running in a tall position with the proper lean, which is very important. The foot plant always seems to be underneath the kneecap so that the center of gravity can rock over the kneecap to facilitate greater leg drive. The head is always in line with the upper torso, and upon close examination, one can see the relaxed facial muscles and the open mouth for relaxed breathing. There is an excellent illustration of arm action through all the pictures. The looseness of the athlete's hands and the unclenched fist, which facilitates relaxation, are especially noteworthy.

4

THE 400m. STRIDE

Athlete: **Monika Zehrt,** *East Germany*

Olympic Competition:
    400m.   1972   1st   51.1 (Olympic Record)

Author: **Nell Jackson** is Associate Professor in the Department of Physical Education for Women at Michigan State University. A former American record-holder in the 200m., and a member of United States Olympic (1948 and 1952) and Pan-American Games (1951) teams, she is one of this country's outstanding coaches of women's events. She has served as manager of the U.S. women's team in Europe (1966), Israel (1967), and Martinique (1971), as a coach of the U.S. women's team at the University World Games (1970), and at the Olympic Games (1972). In addition, she has been Chairman of the A.A.U. Women's Track and Field Committee (1968-1971), the U.S. Women's Olympic Track and Field Committee (1969-1972), and a Member of the Board of Directors of the U.S. Olympic Committee (1969-1972).

Figure 1 The left foot is just completing its supportive phase while the right leg is moving through under the body. As in sprinting, the lower right leg is tucked closely to the thigh causing the leg to be brought through relatively fast. The trunk is in a good upright position. The arms are almost in line with the body and appear to be rather tense. The left arm is moving forward and the right one is moving backward.

Figure 2 The center of gravity of the body continues to move forward and ahead of the left leg. Here, the driving phase is almost complete as the left leg extends and the runner is on the ball of the foot. Even though Zehrt is a powerful runner, it seems as if she may be losing a few extra inches with each stride by not getting as much drive as she could. This is suggested by the partial bend in the left leg. The right knee completes its lift as a reaction to the drive of the left leg. The arms are continuing to move forward and backward from the shoulder. The trunk and head continue to be held in good alignment.

Figure 3 The driving phase has been completed. The center of gravity of the body is near its highest point of the running action with both feet off the ground. Zehrt is in the middle of the recovery phase and the left leg, having completed its drive, begins to flex. As the left arm swings forward it appears to be driving toward the midline of the body. Again, tension appears to be apparent in the tight fist.

Figure 4 The right foot is well in front of the knee and will begin its back and downward movement to the ground, while the lower left leg continues to fold toward the buttocks. The head and trunk are still in good alignment with the rest of the body.

Figure 1   **Figure 2**   **Figure 3**   **Figure 4**

Figure 5 The left leg continues to fold up behind the body moving toward a shorter and faster lever. This is a quality that allows Zehrt to have fast leg action. The amount of the leg fold is a result of the strong drive. The right foot is about to contact the ground with the body's weight going toward the outside of the ball of the foot.

Figure 6 Here again is the supportive phase. The right heel has touched the ground and the knee bends in order for the body to pivot over the foot. The center of gravity of the body is probably at its lower point in the stride. The lower left leg folds tightly toward the hips while the left arm begins to drive backward and the right arm forward. The left leg becomes a short but fast lever moving from the hip.

Figure 7 The trunk is rotating forward over the right foot. This moves right into the driving phase of the stride pattern; the leg is relatively extended and the runner is on the ball of her foot. From the partial flexion of the knee it again appears as if the right leg is lacking some drive. *Note:* This could also mean that the photographer missed the final drive of the leg. The knee is coming through relatively high as a result of the drive of the right leg. The arms are continuing the drive; the right arm appears to be swinging across the chest while the left arm is moving back.

Figure 8 Again, she has reached the middle of the recovery phase. The right foot completes its extension as the lower left leg begins to extend forward. The left arm is swinging back with a more open position. This open back swing balances the long powerful extension of the driving leg.

Figure 9 This is a continuation of the recovery phase. The left foot has now been swung in front of the knee as the right leg begins to fold up

Figure 5   **Figure 6**   **Figure 7**   **Figure 8**

behind the body. Notice the relaxed action of the runner, except for the hands. The trunk and head positions are still good.

Figure 10 The left foot is about to contact the ground and the lower right leg continues to fold up toward the hips. Again, the arms are midway in their swing; it appears as if the left arm has a slight lateral movement while the right arm is swinging across the midline of the body. The thigh development of Zehrt is very typical of today's sprinters.

Figure 11 The left foot has now contacted the ground and the trunk is practically over the supporting foot. The left knee is slightly bent, allowing the body to rotate over the foot. The right foot is tucked closely to the hips. This permits the thigh to come forward relatively fast as a short lever.

Figure 9   **Figure 10**   **Figure 11**

5

THE 800m. STRIDE

Athlete: **Dave Wottle,** *U.S.A.*

Olympic Competition:
    800m.   1972   1st   1:45.9

Author: **Mel Brodt**, track and cross-country coach at Bowling Green State University, Ohio, is one of the leading U.S. authorities on track and cross-country running. Coach of Olympic champion and world-record holder, Dave Wottle, he is currently President of the U.S. Track Coaches Association and Secretary of the U.S. Cross-Country Coaches Association.

47

Undoubtedly this photo sequence was taken during the first 200 meters of the finals of the 800 meters at the 1972 Olympic Games in Munich, Germany. Dave Wottle was pressing to catch up during this sequence, consequently illustrating slightly forced and not relaxed or highly efficient movements. However, he does not appear to be overly anxious or greatly concerned about being behind.

Figure 1 Facial features show no strain or undue tension. The mouth is open with jaw loose and relaxed. His right foot is positioned with toe angled slightly to the right of center (due to Wottle's being knock-kneed).

Figure 2 With the exception of a slight backward tilting of the head, the upper torso demonstrates good body angle with left hand carriage at hip level. Left leg lift shows the lower leg follow through to be efficient. Shoulders are a little tight with the angle of a cocked left wrist indicating a slightly forced arm action.

Figure 3 Lower left leg extension action seems slightly forced here due to position in race while still "building" to attain relaxed rhythm and race pace. Arms show forceful action causing slight shoulder movement to the left—movement is reduced in Figure 8 but still evident.

Figure 4 Left leg extension demonstrates slightly bent knee to absorb any shock upon foot placement. Heel landing shows possible hard

Figure 1   Figure 2   Figure 3

landing; however, it does not cause any retardation of forward movement as seen in Figure 5.

Figure 5 Foot placement appears to be just ahead of the hips, which could tend to inhibit forward momentum. Actual foot landing takes place with the center of gravity almost directly above the foot.

Figure 6 The left leg is flexed as body weight passes in front of the left foot. The lift of the right leg is continued with the left foot beginning to extend for the forward push-off and driving action.

Figure 7 Lift of the right leg with the left leg almost fully extended with the forward drive off the foot demonstrating excellent, efficient push-off. The torso is slightly arched with chest forward and upward for efficient air intake and expulsion.

Figure 8 Length of stride exhibits power driving action which is still in use during this "catch-up" phase of the race. Relaxation is evidenced by his head position (see Figure 3).

Figure 9 Foot placement is definitely on the outside of the right foot which is normal for most middle-distance runners. Rhythm and smoothness is evident here as timing and relaxation is beginning to take place.

Figure 10 Figure 10 illustrates an excellent relaxed phase with a very good angle of the torso. Left leg action is possibly a shade high on

Figure 4   Figure 5   Figure 6

the rear leg kickup; however, this demonstrates a normal follow-through action for Wottle (see Figure 1). Leverage of the leg is shortened as it swings forward providing for better efficiency in leg action.

TRAINING

The following schedules will give some idea of Wottle's actual workouts at the various times throughout the 1972 track season. Upper body weight work was employed for the maintenance of strength twice weekly throughout the indoor season. This training was reduced to once a week in April and mid-May and was then abandoned completely in late May and June for the Championship meets.

All morning workouts were on the roads and streets of the campus, the city of Bowling Green, and the surrounding rural community. An average distance throughout the 12½ month program was 5 miles for every workout taken. These workouts were basically *mental* in nature with volume really being incidental. Our afternoon workouts were preceded with a varied but routine 3-4 mile warm-up and followed with a 2-3 mile rundown. All calisthenics were individually performed according to need with primary emphasis on loosening and stretching exercises. Pick-ups or windsprints with finish-action practice cap off the warm-up.

Figure 7   **Figure 8**

The following weekly workouts are those taken directly from Wottle's log. They are, by no means, to be taken as workouts which are to be used by others with the expectations of becoming a great middle-distance performer.

Schedule 1

(Week No. 6—February 13-19, 1972)

	a.m.	p.m.
Sun.	d.n.r.	10 mi. easy
Mon.	7 mi. easy	4 mi. warm-up; 1320 in 3:48; 1320 at 5:00 pace with 4 accelerations/lap and last 660 at 60 sec pace; 880 at 80 sec base pace with 5 accelerations/lap; 3 mi. rundown.
Tues.	d.n.r.	4 mi. warm-up; 550 at 60 sec pace; 1½ mi. with alternate 100's at good and easy pace; 3 mi. rundown.
Wed.	4 mi. easy	4 mi. warm-up; 2 × 880 Fartlek; 1 mi. at 80 sec base pace wi 3 accelerations/lap; 3 mi. rundown.
Thur.	5 mi. easy	5 mi. easy.

Figure 9

Figure 10

| Fri. | 4 mi. easy | *U.S. Olympic Invitational* (indoor), New York. 1½ mi. warm-up; 1500 m. in 3:44.5; 1½ mi. rundown. |
| Sat. | 2 mi. easy | *Central Collegiates* (indoor) Kalamazoo. 1½ mi. warm-up; 880 in 1:50.6; ½ mi. rundown; 1 mi. warm-up; 2 mi. in 8:59.9; 1 mi. rundown. |

Schedule 2

(Week No. 10—March 5-11, 1972)

	a.m.	p.m.
Sun.	7 mi. easy	d.n.r.
Mon.	7 mi. easy	4 mi. warm-up; 1000 at 70 sec pace; 1 mi. accelerating straights and jogging turns; 2 × 440 (59 and 60); 2 mi. rundown.
Tues.	7 mi. easy	4 mi. warm-up; 440 in 54.5; 660 (440 in 60 sec/220 very brisk); 1320 with alternate 110's accelerating and jogging; 2 mi. rundown.
Wed.	7 mi. easy	4 mi. warm-up; 3 × 330 at 880 pace (good-quick-accelerating); 660 easy; 2 mi. rundown.
Thurs.	d.n.r.	5 mi. easy
Fri.	1½ mi. easy	*N.C.A.A. Championships* (indoor), Detroit. 2 mi. warm-up; 880 in 1:53.6; 1½ mi. rundown; 1½ mi. warm-up; 880 in 1:51.8; 1½ mi. rundown.
Sat.	2½ mi. easy	*N.C.A.A. Championships* (indoor) Detroit. 2 mi. warm-up; Mile (relay) 4:02.3; 1½ mi. rundown.

Schedule 3

(Week No. 19—May 7-14, 1972)

	a.m.	p.m.
Sun.	9 mi. easy	d.n.r.
Mon.	7 mi. easy	3 mi. warm-up; 3 × 1320 at 75 sec pace—1 min. recovery; 4 mi. rundown.
Tues.	5 mi. easy	4 mi. warm-up; 2 × 440 at 59 sec pace with all-out finish; 880 with alternate 100's good and easy; 4 × 440 (63, 62, 60, 55) with 2-3 min. recovery; 3 mi. rundown.

Wed.	7 mi. easy	4 mi. warm-up; 2 × 330 (45 & 42); 220 in 27; 4 × 220 (27, 28, 27, 26) with 220 easy recovery; 880 in 2:06; 880 with alternate 220's good, easy, quick, and driving to finish; 2 mi. rundown.
Thur.	7 mi. easy	4 mi. warm-up; 440 in 61; 660 at 880 pace; 440 at mile pace (mixed paces within 440); 550 at 65 sec pace with 5 accelerations/ lap; 2 mi. rundown.
Fri.	5 mi. easy	6 mi. Fartlek
Sat.	3½ mi. easy	*Triangular.* 1 mi. warm-up; 880 in 1:52.4; 1 mi. rundown; 1 mi. easy.
Sun.	1½ mi. easy	*M.L. King Freedom Games*, Philadelphia. 2 mi. warm-up; 1 mi. in 3:58.5; 2 mi. rundown.

Schedule 4

(Week No. 22—May 28-June 3, 1972)

	a.m.	p.m.
Sun.	d.n.r.	4 mi. easy
Mon.	5 mi. easy	5 mi. easy with middle 2 mi. at 5:00 pace
Tues.	5 mi. easy	3 mi. warm-up; 440 in 57; 3 × 220 (29, 27, 26) with 220 recovery jog; 1100 at 70 sec pace; 2½ mi. rundown.
Wed.	5 mi. easy	3 mi. easy
Thur.	1 mi. easy	*N.C.A.A. Championships, Eugene.* 3 mi. warm-up; 1500 heat in 3:46.9; 3 mi. rundown.
Fri.	5 mi. easy	d.n.r.
Sat.	1 mi. easy	*N.C.A.A. Championships, Eugene.* 3 mi. warm-up; 1500 final in 3:39.7; 2 mi. rundown.

Schedule 5

(Weeks 26-28—June 18-July 8, 1972)*

	a.m.	p.m.
Sun.	d.n.r.	6½ mi. easy
Mon.	6 mi. easy	2 mi. easy
Tues.	8 mi. easy	d.n.r.

*Ran 3 races in A.A.U. Championships June 15, 16, & 17 (Won 800 in 1:47.3).

Wed.	8 mi. easy	4 mi. warm-up; 440 in 72; 880 in 2:20; 2 × 1 mi. (4:38, 4:48); 2 × 440 with alternate 55's very good and easy; 10 × 120 very good; 3 mi. rundown.
Thur.	8 mi. easy	d.n.r.
Fri.	8 mi. easy	3 mi. warm-up; 8 x 100—beginning of race; 1¾ in 7:46 (67, 70, 71, 70, 64, 64, 60); 1320 with consecutive 55's and 100's easy and accelerating; 3 mi. rundown.
Sat.	7 mi. easy	3 mi. warm-up; 4 × 440 (mixed paces); 2 × 440 in 59 and 61; 550 at 61 sec pace and building; 3 × 440 with consecutive 110's easy, good, brisk and accelerating; 3 mi. rundown.
Sun.	d.n.r.	8½ mi. easy
Mon.	6 mi. easy	2 mi. warm-up; 3 × 440 (56.5, 56, 55) with full recovery; 4 mi. rundown.
Tues.	5 mi. easy	3 mi. easy (travel)
Wed.	d.n.r.	4½ mi. easy
Thur.	2½ mi. easy	*U.S. Olympic Trials, Eugene.* 2½ mi. warm-up; 800 heat in 1:49.8; 2 mi. rundown.
Fri.	3 mi. easy	*U.S. Olympic Trials, Eugene.* 2½ mi. warm-up; 800 semi in 1:47.4; 3 mi. rundown.
Sat.	1 mi. easy	*U.S. Olympic Trials, Eugene.* 2½ mi. warm-up; 800 final in 1:44.3; 2½ mi. rundown.
Sun.	d.n.r.	6 mi. easy.
Mon.	6 mi. easy	3 mi. warm-up; 150 at 60 sec pace—jog 290; 2 × 440 (56.8, 58.5); 1100 (69, 100 brisk, 110 easy, 56.5 with 3 accelerations per lap); 4 × 220 (27.9, 28, 28, 28.4); 3 mi. rundown.
Tues.	5 mi. easy	5 mi. easy
Wed.	5 mi. easy	d.n.r.
Thur.	1½ mi. easy	*U.S. Olympic Trials, Eugene.* 2½ mi. warm-up; 1500 heat in 3:43.7; 2 mi. rundown.
Fri.	1 mi. easy	*U.S. Olympic Trials, Eugene.* 2½ mi. warm-up; 1500 semi in 3:44.7; 1½ mi. rundown.
Sat.	1 mi. easy	*U.S. Olympic Trials, Eugene.* 2½ mi. warm-up; 1500 final in 3:42.3; 2 mi. rundown.

6

THE 1500m. STRIDE

Athlete: **Ludmila Bragina**, *U.S.S.R.*

Olympic Competition:
    1500m.   1972   1st   4:01.4 (World Record)

Author: **Enrique Eleusippi**, the former head coach of the Argentine national team (1963), has studied track and field in the U.S.A. (1964) and in Germany (1970). He is currently Technical Advisor of the Argentine Athletic Union, and Editor of *Stadium*, a South American publication for coaches and physical educators.

Figure 1 Nearing completion of the recovery phase, Ludmila Bragina's left foot is coming to the ground.

Figure 2 Contact has been made first on the outside edge of the foot, with toes pointing slightly outward. Then the left foot receives the full weight of her body at a point that depends on the runner's speed.

Figure 3 The driving phase is now beginning; her general body position as well as the action of the arms and legs is perfectly balanced, and shows good coordination. Her head, however, is not in good alignment. It is rather low, and facing the ground.

Figure 4 Bragina is completing a stride on her left foot. Her right leg is almost reaching its highest point.

Figure 5 The left leg is completely extended and the right knee is in maximum lift. The arms swing in a relaxed but powerful fashion. The

Figure 1 **Figure 2** **Figure 3** **Figure 4**

Figure 8 **Figure 9** **Figure 10** **Figure 11**

trunk is almost in a vertical position and the front leg is moving forward in a smooth and natural way.

Figure 6 Both feet are off the ground. Her right elbow has reached the limit point moving to the rear.

Figure 7 The lead leg is going to make contact with a slightly flexed right knee. Bragina is well balanced: arms, trunk and legs are in good position.

Figure 8 Her right foot has made contact with the ground by the ball, just ahead of her center of gravity.

Figure 9 The slight bending of her right knee has assured a comfortable landing. The body is moving over her right foot, the full sole of the foot is in contact with the ground. The left knee is moving up and forward.

Figure 5   **Figure 6**   **Figure 7**

Figure 12   **Figure 13**   **Figure 14**

Figure 10 The center of gravity is also moving forward and her rear leg is beginning to apply its driving force towards the body. Arms are moving backward and forward in a very relaxed and quiet manner.

Figure 11 She is now completing a stride on her right foot as the front leg reaches the correct limit of its forward swing.

Figure 12 The driving phase has been completed; all extensions end together with the foot pointing, once again, slightly outward and breaking contact with its inside front edge. The arms are absorbing the reaction to the leg thrust. The recovery phase is beginning again.

Figures 13–14 Continuation of the recovery phase. The cycle begun in Figure 1 is completed in Figure 14.

TRAINING

Bragina began her training for Munich in November 1971 in the Caucasus at an elevation of 5,000 feet (1700 m.) with long runs of about an hour. Subsequently she trained at sea level.

She trains twice a day, five times per week and runs up to 19 miles (30 km.) per day. In the mornings (around 7 a.m.) she runs the same distance as at midday (around 1 p.m.). Her afternoon runs are significantly faster. Besides fast long runs of 9-10 miles (15-16 km.) she also runs series of 10 × 800m., 10 × 100m., or 10 × 1200m.

7

THE 5,000-10,000m. STRIDE

Athlete: **Lasse Viren,** *Finland*

Olympic Competition:

5,000m.	1972	1st	13:26.4 (Olympic Record)
10,000m.	1972	1st	27:38.4 (World Record)

The Author: **Kalevi Römpötti**, former national coach of Finland (1948-52) and Professor of track and field in the Physical Education Institute of Helsinki University (1953-70), is currently Head of the Armed Forces Physical Education Office in Helsinki. Author of *How to Run Victories and Records* (1973) and numerous technical articles on track and field, he is also a Board Member of the International Track and Field Coaches Association and Chairman of the coaching section of the International Military Sports Council.

Figure 1   Figure 2   Figure 3

Lasse Viren, one of the finest products of the Finnish school of running, is the ideal type of endurance runner in terms of psycho-physical make-up. Born in 1949, he is 5 feet 11 inches (180 cm.) tall, extremely light in build, 132 pounds (60 kg.), and has a sinewy strength. He is a natural talent with awesome tenacity and is unshakingly unruffled and well-balanced. Tactically, he is a most intelligent runner.

To date, Viren's biggest successes have been his victories in the 5,000 and 10,000 meters at the Olympics in Munich in 1972. In that year he also established world records at 2 miles (8:14.0), 5,000m. (13:16.4) and 10,000m. (27:38.4).

Figure 7   Figure 8   Figure 9

Figure 4   **Figure 5**   **Figure 6**

Viren runs with an extremely economical, balanced, yet rather short and speedy stride which is admirably rhythmical and relaxed.

Figures 1, 8 and 14 Viren's landing is economical and sparing on his calf muscles; his heel is leading slightly and his instep is directly forward. This point marks the start of the preparatory phase during which the runner's center of gravity moves forward over the grounded foot (fulcrum). The forward lean of the body facilitates this movement. This lean of Viren's is a very advantageous one.

Figures 2, 9 and 15 During the preparatory phase the runner gets ready—as a reflex, not consciously—for the drive into the next stride. The runner, as it were, "collapses" limply over the supporting leg. The

Figure 10   **Figure 11**   **Figure 12**

Figure 13   **Figure 14**

pelvis drops slightly lower, the knee bends and the whole body of the runner gets ''charged'' for the drive.

Figures 3, 10 and 16 The drive begins the moment the runner's center of gravity reaches a position above the fulcrum. This is the moment at which the crown of the runner's head is at its lowest, and the angles of pelvis, knee, and ankle are at their sharpest. Sideways, too, the runner is leaning over the supporting foot, so that the body's center of gravity comes directly above the driving foot.

Figures 4, 5 and 11 Viren's drive is just being made. The drive is aided, in reflex, by the relaxed forward and upward swing of the free leg. Viren pulls his free leg forwards economically, from a very low position.

Figure 15   **Figure 16**

Figures 6 & 12 Viren's drive has ended with a full extension of pelvis, knee, and ankle. At this moment, the runner is in an extreme position. The crown of the head is at its highest point, the knee of the free leg is in the extreme position backwards-and-upwards and forwards-and-upwards.

Figures 7 & 13 After the drive Viren is shot into the air. During one step a middle-distance runner is in the air for roughly the same length of time as he is in contact with the ground. For instance, a 10,000 meter runner who achieves a time of 28 minutes is in the air for about 14 minutes of this time. It is consequently by no means a matter of indifference how that time in the air is spent. The best opportunity for reflexive relaxation occurs then. The legs swing towards each other. The thigh of the forward leg drops. Concurrently the shin swings forward in a relaxed way. When the leg has almost straightened out, the whole leg swings downwards and backwards in a relaxed manner. The hands also swing towards each other, forwards-and-downwards and backwards-and-downwards.

GENERAL OBSERVATIONS ON VIREN'S RUNNING

Due to the brevity of his stride, Viren's work with his hands and the opposed rotations of the pelvis and shoulder lines are somewhat limited. All superfluous movements have been eliminated in his extremely economical action. Viren carries his arms tightly coiled and rather high, in the same way as did Zatopek or Kuts, for instance. The use of the hands, as with all running, is something highly individual. In long-distance running the most important thing is to find a way of carrying the arms so that they will seem to weigh as little as possible. Yet a long-distance runner must also have a command of the sprinter's arm action, to which he must resort in his final dash and overtaking spurts.

Viren's head does not bob (like those of Zatopek, Gammoudi or Ryun) but stays put, with the glance being directed firmly at the track as if keeping a watch on a point running away a few strides ahead. This helps him to maintain an extremely relaxed and balanced action. With the aid of his glance Viren also retains his very favorable body lean. Notice, too, the concentrated and determined facial expression.

TEACHING RUNNING TECHNIQUES

Children learn to run at an age of 2-3 years. So when teaching the techniques of running the question is not one of teaching anything new but rather of correcting any faults. An economic technique of running should be taught as early as possible. Children of 7-9 years can be taught to run in an extremely relaxed way, with gentle noiselessness and with a rhythmical balance. (Do not stalk or leap. Instead, run with short and rapid strides.) Normally when the running action looks beautiful it is also technically correct.

Primarily on account of differences in anatomical structure, the technique of running is something highly individual. There is no reason to be dogmatic in teaching the techniques. The former Finnish coach Armas Valste would no more have considered the heel step of Viren with favor than Arthur Lydiard favors Viren's high carriage of the arms.

Many coaches in Finland and elsewhere are of the opinion that "you learn to run only by running." This opinion is wrong. If your young protégé tenses up when running, watch how he walks. You will find that he "tenses up" when he is walking too. Only after learning to relax in his everyday walking, can he learn to run in a relaxed way. If your protégé runs with a leaping or bounding motion watch how he walks. You will notice that he does the same when he walks. Not before he has learned to walk with a shorter and quicker stride will he learn to run in a more economical fashion. And if your athlete happens to run with his ankles turned sharply outwards, you can be sure that you will find the same fault in his walk. Anyone who intends to become a really good runner should make his every walking step serve his running. Watch how Lasse Viren walks and you will have a better understanding of why he is one of the world's best runners today.

TRAINING

There is nothing unusual or sensational about Viren's training. He trains year round and covers approximately 120 miles per week when in full training. Aerobic (with oxygen) endurance, anerobic (without oxygen) endurance, and speed are each given appropriate emphasis during the course of his total preparation for competitive racing. His workouts do not follow the "cultist" pattern advocated by some internationally-renowned coaches, but rather they reveal common sense in terms of variety and mixture of distances and speed.

8

THE MARATHON

Athlete: **Frank Shorter,** *U.S.A. (#1014)*

Olympic Competition:

10,000m.	1972	5th	27:51.4
Marathon	1972	1st	2:12:19.8

Author: **Roy Benson** is assistant track and cross-country coach at the University of Florida. He is a former National Advisory Coach to the Phillipines Olympic team (1971-72).

To say that Frank Shorter is an ex-
tremely efficient running machine is to state the obvious. However, the
reasons for this may not be quite so obvious, and the purpose of this
analysis is to explore two factors that appear to be at least partially
responsible for his effectiveness.

The most important aspect of Shorter's form is that he carries himself in the ideal running position from a mechanical viewpoint. Much of
the credit for this near-perfect form must go to Shorter's former Yale
coach, Bob Giegengack, who was responsible for helping him develop
correct body carriage. Shorter does not waste energy pushing himself
back up from a falling position caused by running with a forward lean.
Naturally, the reverse is true because he does not run with a backward
lean either. All of his energy goes into the production of forward thrust.
As Bill Bowerman of Oregon would say, "Shorter runs tall."

The other aspect of Shorter's form become apparent through longitudinal analysis of his career. This is a significant reduction in body
weight from around 140 pounds as an undergraduate to around 130
pounds in his present condition. Although this weight loss is not dramatic
enough to catch the attention of the "Weight Watchers," close observation of pictures taken over the last four years reveals how much Shorter's
running regime has reduced his body musculature to only that which is
absolutely essential to an efficient running style. This reduction of body
weight is probably one reason why Shorter gives the impression of having
a feathery, light stride. (Indeed, at 5 feet 11 inches [1.80 m.] and 130
pounds [58.8 kg.], he does resemble a feather.)

Dr. Ernst Van Aaken has worked at considerable length with
theories regarding body weight and power-to-weight ratios. As he points
out, by reducing not only body fat, but also nonessential muscle tissue,
one can increase his average pace. This is possible since the body's work
load is reduced (i.e. it's easier to carry a lighter load) and also because
there are fewer oxygen-consuming tissues on the body frame. As additional research has shown, a 5 percent reduction in body fat can mean as
much as a 5 percent increase in maximum oxygen uptake. If this holds
true, then Shorter's missing 10 pounds, which constitute about 7 percent
weight reduction, might perhaps mean a corresponding increase of 7
percent in his maximum oxygen uptake. Unfortunately, no laboratory
research has been done on Shorter, so there is no evidence to either
support or deny this suggestion—a suggestion that is certainly worth
considering.

The Marathon

TRAINING

Pre-race warmup: Jog 3 miles at near 8 min/mile pace; stretching and then strides; jog approximately 1 mile. Possibly some short, fast runs if the competition is a fast track race.

Pre-training warmup: Prior to interval training, same as race routine. Before long distance runs, 3 mile jog.

Training: Shorter's training remains essentially the same the year round. In the morning Shorter usually runs 7-10 miles at 9:00-10:00 a.m. on grass or roads, at a pace of 6:30-7:00 minutes per mile. When not competing, he runs 15-20 miles on grass or road, four evenings each week at a speed often well below 6:00 minutes per mile. Three evenings each week are devoted to intense interval-training, using fast repetitions with short recovery jogging between. His most severe interval-training workout is 15 x 440 yards, jogging 50 yards after each. These are usually run in 62-64 seconds. On one occasion he averaged 61 seconds on these fifteen 440's and completed the final quarter in 58 seconds! Shorter runs an average of 140-150 miles each week, and has occasionally covered 170 miles in seven days. A compulsive runner, Shorter does not rest prior to racing. However, he eases his running volume prior to a marathon. He has experimented with lifting light weights in recent years since graduating from Yale in 1969. Shorter has an amazing tolerance for heat, and is one of the most talented athletes ever to compete at the marathon distance. He is a law student at the University of Florida in Gainesville, where he resides with his wife, Louise Gilliland, whom he married in 1971. He was coached at Yale by Bob Giegengack. He has had no "coach" as such since then.

9

THE STEEPLECHASE WATER JUMP

Athlete: **Kipchoge Keino**, *Kenya*

Olympic Competition:

1500m.	1968	1st	3:34.9
			(Olympic Record)
5000m.	1968	2nd	14:05.2
3000m.	1972	1st	8:23.6
Steeplechase			(Olympic Record)
1500m.	1972	2nd	3:36.8

Author: **Denis Watts**, Principle National Coach for Great Britain, is one of a long line of outstanding British coaches of track and field. Coach of British Olympic teams (1964, 1968 and 1972) and English Commonwealth Games teams (1958, 1962 and 1970), he has also served as Head Coach of the British Commonwealth team vs. U.S.A. (1967) and Coach of the European team vs. the Americas (1969). A former British international in the long and triple jumps, and the author of no less than ten books on track and field, he has personally coached four Olympic medallists.

This series of pictures shows Kip-choge Keino clearing the water jump during the Olympic Games in Munich.

The technique of water jumping can make a tremendous difference to the entire race. If the water jump is negotiated badly, fatigue can make itself felt early. The physical effort of picking up the speed of the race again after tumbling out of the water can turn possible victory into certain defeat.

Figures 1–3 Keino's speed will increase slightly as he approaches the hurdle in order to obtain a satisfactory clearance. The take-off spot has fallen some 4½-5 feet (1.37-1.52 m.) from the hurdle and depends upon personal judgment brought about by experience.

Figures 4–7 The ball of the foot is placed on the rail. Good steeple-chase shoes have small spikes placed on the instep in order to assist in

Figure 1   **Figure 2**   **Figure 3**

Figure 7   **Figure 8**   **Figure 9**

obtaining an immediate purchase in the wooden rail. These become increasingly valuable to the runner as the rail begins to get wet after many athletes have crossed the barrier. Keino's body is lowered so that he may pivot easily over his foot which is placed on the rail. He now passes through a crouched·position from which he can push off to clear the water.

Figures 8–11 Generally the stronger leg is placed on the rail of the barrier, in this case, Keino's right leg. This is the driving leg and it should continue to push against the rail for as long as possible. This leads to a good split between the legs and the athlete will come down into a normal running action straight out of the water. In effect, the instruction given to the athlete should be "Keep the foot against the rail for as long as possible."

Figures 12–13 Note that the drive off the rail is *out* and not *up*.

Figure 4   **Figure 5**   **Figure 6**

Figure 10   **Figure 11**   **Figure 12**

Although Keino is landing right on the edge of the water, most athletes are content to land in about 6 inches (15cm.) of water. In other words they get one foot wet and, in doing so, obtain a satisfactory compromise between jumping too far which is too fatiguing and falling too short into the water. The latter makes even further demands on energy reserves in struggling out of deep water and means that the runner interrupts his running in order to pick up speed following each clearance.

Figures 14–18 In this case Keino has slightly over-reached himself in attempting to go too far. This would explain the irregular arm action (they are being used as balancers) and the rather off-balance landing and first stride out of the water. However, for a man blessed with his powers of endurance this technique is acceptable and the results are there to prove it.

Figure 13   **Figure 14**   **Figure 15**

Figure 16   **Figure 17**   **Figure 18**

10

THE HIGH HURDLES

Athlete: **Rod Milburn,** *U.S.A.*

Olympic Competition:
    110m. Hurdles   1972   1st   13.2 (World Record)

Author: **Jagmohan Singh**, a former national record holder in the high hurdles and decathlon, represented India in the 110m. hurdles at the Olympic Games (1960) and served as Coach of the Indian track and field team at the British Commonwealth Games (1966). A member of the teaching staff at the National Institute of Sports, Patiala, he is responsible for instruction in sprints, hurdles and relays at that institution. He is also National Coach for sprints and hurdles.

Figure 1 The action is a stride be-
fore take off. It gives the impression that an effort is being made in
preparation for take off. If examined carefully it can be compared with the
gathering phase of a jumper. Perhaps the last stride is being shortened a
bit. One fault which is magnified later in the form of a locked lead leg
(Figure 5) arises here—possibly due to a slight tension of the ankle joint
resulting in a negligible stretch of the foot. Such action can easily be
correlated with an early opening of the knee of the lead leg during knee
pick-up.

Figure 2 Figure 2 illustrates the start of the take off movement. The
position of the hurdler differs somewhat from that of a sprinter. The body
has moved slightly forward in preparation for the leap and this has resulted in a slight upper body lean even at this early stage of the take off.
The left arm has undergone necessary adjustment for the desired upper
body bend and shifting of center of gravity in relation to the take-off
point. This anticipated shift in center of gravity accelerates the pivoting
action and hence helps in achieving the forward rotation which is absolutely essential for quick hurdle clearance and early landing.

Figure 3 A fraction of a second before contact with the ground is
broken and the left knee is not yet fully stretched. The pivoting action has
started and as a result, the heel of the take-off foot has come up and the
body weight rests on the ball of the foot. Although the knee joint of the
driving leg has been extended there is no appreciable rise in the head
position. This ensures a step-over action rather than a sailing action over

Figure 1   **Figure 2**   **Figure 3**

the barrier. The lead leg knee is being picked up and the left arm is moving upward rather than forward with the elbow being lifted upward and sideward. The right arm moves forward rather than backward reflecting a tendency towards use of the double-arm action.

There is a slight early opening of the forward lead leg that indicates not only a knee pick-up action but a positive action of the fore leg. The angle at the knee joint is very close to 90 degrees although the thigh has not yet reached the horizontal position. This premature opening of the lead leg slows down the knee pick-up action to some extent. In fact, the foreleg should not cross the vertical plane before the take-off action is completed (i.e. before ground contact is lost). If it does, this leads to a jumping action because of the increased vertical component in the forces applied for the leap. Timely opening of the lead leg accelerates the free knee pick-up and also ensures a better leg split at the take off.

Figure 4 Immediately after take-off the upper part of the lead leg is parallel to the ground but the foreleg has moved well ahead of the knee which has been opened up much more than it should be. This action adds to the vertical lift and reduces the vital forward rotation. The head has been lifted a little higher than in Figure 3. This shows clearly the tendency towards a slight jumping effect. In the case of hurdlers who obtain a good split and a controlled opening of the lead leg, the head does not go up—even if they do not adopt the eyes down/head down position over the hurdle.

Figure 5 The premature opening of the foreleg results in a locking

Figure 4   **Figure 5**

of the knee of the lead leg. This locked knee position of the leg checks the body lean to some extent. The left elbow is being lifted up higher than the head. Such an action, although it does not hamper relaxation, may result in a comparatively straight arm pull-back action. The palm of the hand is facing forward and sideways rather than downward due to excessive lift of the elbow, and this position of the palm is mainly responsible for the wide swing of the left arm in its backward movement (Figures 8-9). The right arm does not come up high enough and hence the right shoulder drops.

Figure 6 The momentary locking of the lead leg is over and there is a clear bend at the knee. This is a favorable position for the upper body bend and has resulted in a narrowing of the angle between the lead leg thigh and the trunk as compared to that in Figure 5. The front foot has started the landing action. This is quite clear from the position of the foot which is in a somewhat stretched position. As the trail knee is being pulled forward the left arm has started moving down in the first stage of its backward movement.

Figure 7 The results of the slightly early opening of the lead knee (Figure 3) and the resulting comparatively poor leg split (Figure 4) are evident here. The trail leg seems to have caught up with the lead leg and the hurdler is in a somewhat cramped position. The trail knee is already ahead of the hip even before the hip comes over the hurdle bar. This is a position which is unlike those of other top-class hurdlers.

A very good action is demonstrated by Milburn in Figures 6-7.

Figure 6   Figure 7

Although the lead leg has opened up a little early, the action of the trail leg is a perfect pulling-without-lifting action. This checks the tendency of the jumping action to a great extent. The body lean is maintained with body weight well forward. This body lean (along with the forward rotation created at the take off) facilitates a quick landing. The left arm has moved on its backward path. There is no significant lowering of the head position which normally is the case with top-class hurdlers at this point. This lower position is obtained through a good split and forward rotation at the take off.

The insufficient knee pick-up at the take off is reflected here in the faulty low position of the lead foot over the top of the hurdle. The hurdle has been hit most probably with the heel of the lead foot—something which is very uncommon with good hurdlers. If there is a sufficient knee pick-up the foot will cross fairly well above the bar of the hurdle.

Figure 8 The hurdler is looking at the next hurdle which, in my opinion, is better for field survey and the maintenance of balance than the eyes-down position. The lead leg has moved well ahead of the hurdle for landing. The trail knee has moved ahead and has crossed the hurdle top while the corresponding hip is still behind. A very good point is that the fore leg of the trail leg is pulled over the hurdle horizontally. The left arm which has been kept bent throughout has started opening up during its backward, side swinging movement.

Figure 9 The knee is being raised to make room for the rear foot clearance. The hurdler has crossed the hurdle and the left foot is tucked

Figure 8   **Figure 9**

properly so as to avoid hitting the hurdle. The left arm is almost straight as it swings around and has pulled the left shoulder out of line slightly. In fact the entire shoulder girdle seems to have twisted with the right shoulder coming slightly ahead and down. The lowered arm position has added to the lowering of the right shoulder.

Figure 10 There is a timely correction in the wide left arm swing after it crosses the lateral plane of the body. The right leg, which is well ahead of its downward path, is still bent at the knee. This is rather unusual when compared to the actions of other top-class hurdlers. Perhaps the slight imbalanced position of a hurdler hampers a deliberately quicker landing action. The lead leg gets into a locked position much earlier if intentional efforts for landing are made. The trail knee is being picked up high under the arm pit so as to facilitate the achieving of a sound landing position and a good first stride.

Figure 11 The landing is made on the high ball of the foot with a locked knee position which ensures an early touchdown and cuts short the parabolic path followed by the hurdler's center of gravity. The hurdler has assumed a beautiful landing position with a weight distribution such that his center of gravity is well ahead of the point of ground contact. The hips are almost over the foot and the lead leg in a vertical position with upper body bend still maintained. The trail knee is picked up high and brought in front of the chest. Such a landing position, in which there can be no retardation, is very beneficial for a quick getaway into the running strides.

The left arm is bent at almost 90 degrees and this is helpful in

Figure 10   **Figure 11**   **Figure 12**

checking any further twist of the upper body developed through the backward movement of the left arm and the dropping of the right arm too low (Figure 9).

The twist of the upper body and the right shoulder drop during flight result in a little "cross landing." This is quite evident if the take-off and landing marks are compared. The take-off foot is placed to the extreme right side of the lane although he uses a left foot take off. If this point is compared to the point of landing, one finds that the latter is more towards the inside of the lane instead of slightly more to the outside. Possibly this is due to the twist of the upper body and the dropping of the right shoulder.

Figure 12 The trailing leg is not being allowed to drop too early and this will ensure that the hurdler gets a long first stride. The muscular tension clearly shows the vigorous effort to obtain acceleration.

11

THE INTERMEDIATE HURDLES

Athlete: **John Akii-Bua,** *Uganda*

Olympic Competition:
    400m. Hurdles   1972   1st   47.8 (World Record)

Author: **Awoture Eleyae**, a former Nigerian record-holder in the 880 yards and a holder of the British A.A.A. coaching award in hurdles, sprints and relays, was Assistant Coach of the British Commonwealth team vs. U.S.A. (1967) and Head Coach of the Pan-African team vs. U.S.A. (1971). He has also served as Head Coach of the Nigerian track and field team at the All-Africa Games (1965, 1973), the British Commonwealth Games (1966, 1970), the Little Olympics (1967), and the Olympic Games (1968).

81

In undertaking the analysis of the action photographs of John Akii-Bua's hurdling action a number of vital factors that contribute to the totality of the movements can only be presumed. Some of these factors are: the movements of parts of his body which cannot be clearly discerned in a still photograph; the relationship of his total hurdling action to the lane in which he runs; the relationship of his lead leg to his running path, particularly at the curves; and the position of his lead and trailing legs as they contact the track after hurdle clearance.

Figure 1 The photograph shows a normal supporting phase of a sprinting stride. The recovery foot is crossing underneath the body with

Figure 1   **Figure 2**

the heel of the supporting foot almost touching the ground. The body weight is taken on the ball of the supporting foot. The knee of the supporting leg is slightly flexed as a reaction to the alignment of the pelvic girdle which is affected by a lowering of the hip on the side of the recovery leg. This action enables his hips to be square to the direction of run. It also allows the foot to settle down to effect a more forceful drive against the ground. This flexion at the knee also reduces the moment of inertia about the support foot. The knee of the recovery leg is in an effective forward-upward direction. This is the beginning of the approach stride to the hurdle; and it is a good technique to lead this movement with the knee. Even at this early stage there is a slight lean of the upper body, almost 75 degrees. In this position the force of the reaction of the supporting foot to project the body's center of gravity is advantageous. The arms are poised and relaxed, with the shoulders square to the running direction. It would seem as if Akii-Bua hunched his back, but this is only seemingly so, because of the flexed supporting knee preparatory to the driving phase (Figure 2). His eyes seem to be directed beyond the hurdle nearest to him onto the second as if to say, "My next target is not the next hurdle." It is difficult to determine how near to the hurdle he is at this phase.

Figure 3   **Figure 4**

Figure 2 This is an ideal hurdling form for the 400m. intermediate hurdles. The forward lean of 60 degrees is good enough for his height and for the height of the hurdles. The left foot, in its final contact with the ground, looks powerful in its driving phase. The knee of this leg is straightened as compared with what it was in Figure 1. A straight line drawn from the ball of his foot and through his temple passes very close to (if not through) his center of gravity. Since the line of flight is determined at the take off of each stride, this stride of Akii-Bua's becomes effectively crucial. The position of the body's center of gravity over the hurdle can be guessed from the position and direction of his stride. The knee of his lead leg is still in its forward-upward direction. Evidently, the right knee is leading the "assault" on the hurdle. The left shoulder appears to be too high and tight. As a result of this high left shoulder the head has tilted to the right side. This may be only a temporary action. But if it is repetitive at this phase of each hurdle approach, then it will be dysfunctional. In good hurdling the hurdler should drive low relative to the height of the hurdles. A really fast leading leg, therefore, is an asset to good hurdle clearance as this will help to produce the necessary split of the thighs and thus allow the body to dip low. This can be judged from the subsequent

Figure 5   **Figure 6**

photographs. At this stage of the run, the position of the opposite arm to the swinging leg is powerful and it can almost be surmised that the flexed arm is ready to drive forward simultaneously with the leg, in order to act as a stabilizer to the trunk that could be affected by the violent action of the lead leg.

Figure 3 The driving left foot has broken contact with the track; the ankle is relaxed, the knee is flexed and is in the process of rotating. The knee of the lead leg has reached its highest point, and from this time on its height will be determined by the inclination of the trunk and lower leg. The lead leg has started to extend as the foot is directed toward the top of the hurdle. The body lean is still pronounced, and in this ''air-borne'' stage the lean will become more noticeable. To make the trunk lean advantageous to the whole movement, the opposite arm to the lead leg moves forward to counter the reaction of the lead leg on the trunk. In effect, a fast arm action stimulates a fast lead leg, and all (leg and arm) should be directed along the line of running. Since it requires a lot of joint mobility to do this effectively, it can be presumed that Akii-Bua is flexible. This forward thrust of the arm enables the shoulders to be kept square to the direction of the run. It could be adduced that the strong efficient

Figure 7   Figure 8

drive in Figure 2 has contributed to the magnificent leg split which is an essential ingredient of good hurdling. Even with the two feet off the ground and with the lower part of the lead leg still rising the center of gravity does not seem to have risen to any considerable degree. The external rotation, coupled with flexion at knee, ankle and hip are preparatory deviations that facilitate adequate clearance of the hurdle. It recognizes the action toward the hurdle and across the hurdle which must be similar to a normal sprinting stride and, consequently, the alterations needed for purposes of hurdle clearance should not deviate too drastically from the normal running action. The neck seems tense and the head is slightly too high.

Figure 4 Once off the ground, the take-off leg continues to flex—a process started in Figure 3. The knee of Akii-Bua's left leg has flexed to almost 90 degrees whereas his lead leg continues to straighten——approximately 160 degrees. Compared to Figure 2 which shows the last contact he made with the ground, the position of his center of gravity is approximately the same. His left arm has extended almost to the same extent as the lead leg. His shoulders are square to the direction of run. One surprising phenomenon in this photo is the height of his head. Com-

Figure 9   **Figure 10**

pared to Figure 1 in which the supporting leg is slightly flexed, the head height is about the same. This is vital in hurdling as it accounts for economy of effort.

Although the lead leg clearance seems slightly too high above the hurdle, the drive as can be judged from the trail leg is directed horizontally, and will just make for safe clearance of the trail leg at the appropriate time.

Figure 5 The foot of the trailing leg is raised to the level of the center of gravity. The foot is being everted, the knee and the whole of the trailing leg are externally rotated. Flexion of the knee has reduced from 90 to almost 65 degrees. One point of interest at this stage is the position of the lead leg. The knee that was extended to about 160 degrees in Figure 4 has been reduced to almost 155 degrees in this photo. The lower leg is descending and this accounts for the plantar flexion of the right foot. His shoulders are still square to the direction of run. The trunk is still low but the center of gravity seems to have reached its highest point—a few inches higher than his normal running stance as indicated in Figure 2. This highest point of the center of gravity, which is slightly in front of the hurdle, accounts for his lead leg descending in this photo. This is a very sound hurdling tendency as long as it is accompanied by a good forward body lean and other attributes. The arm maintains its extended position with the head relaxed and directed forward.

Figure 6 For a 400m. hurdler, Akii-Bua shows fantastic hurdling form in this photograph. The extension of his lead leg as he descends is comparable only to that in the driving phase in Figure 2. Here the right knee extension approximates 177 degrees. But more outstanding is the position of the trail leg: the left foot is fully everted to clear the hurdle. Here the action of the maintained forward lean finds its reaction in the raising of the left lower leg to clear the hurdle. The split shown in Figures 3-6 is indicative of how flexible Akii-Bua is at the hip, the knee, and the ankle. Although the head seems to be at its highest point in this photo, his center of gravity has dropped below the level it was at in Figure 5. The lateral swing of his left arm is noticeable. It is not clear whether the elbow of his left arm is swinging upward-backward as is likely to be the case in high hurdling. However, the lateral-backward motion of this arm prepares for the pulling through of the trailing knee. His shoulders are still square to the direction of run and his head is still generally in alignment with the shoulders, although he tends to "poke his chin." Ideally, the trailing leg must pass over the hurdle with knee and hip in line. This is what Akii-Bua's position in this picture shows.

Figure 7 He is still air-borne. His leading foot is relaxed with eventual effect on the flexion of his lead knee which has decreased from an angle of 177 to about 160 degrees. The left knee reaches its fullest flexion and highest point while the left foot is still fully everted. Internal rotation has started at the left hip to bring the left knee into a normal sprinting position. There is still great effort to retain the forward lean of the trunk. With his left arm moving back accordingly, Akii-Bua looks well balanced at this stage, quite ready for a smooth landing. The trailing leg has passed the critical phase, and while the everted foot is descending the knee is moving forward and upward. The head is slightly ahead of the shoulders. On the whole, the hurdle action at this stage is good.

Figure 8 The right foot touches down in a pawing manner. His alighting on the ball of the foot makes for balance and a quick getaway. The leg is almost fully extended—about 175 degrees. The foot of the trailing leg is now pulled tightly underneath the buttocks. It is clearly moving from a lateral into a forward position. The knee, which is fully flexed, is also approaching a normal forward position which is characteristic of the driving phase of a sprinting stride.

Probably one of the best features of Akii-Bua's hurdling action can be seen in this photograph. The trunk lean which is still noticeable in this picture is being increased as he rotates further forward and downward. It should be remembered that what is happening here results from what was started in Figure 2, and which was maintained in Figure 4. If the trunk is vertical its moment of inertia about a vertical axis will be relatively small and as a result the shoulders will be vigorously swung which would have affected the forward thrust of the leading arm. But Akii-Bua's trunk in Figures 4-5 is low in relation to the horizontal and hence the greater the moment of intertia about a vertical axis. This presumes less movement in the trunk, which makes it easier for him to keep his shoulders square to the direction of run. What is seen in this picture is a result of previous good mechanical positions of the body. By keeping the body lean across the hurdle and pulling the trailing leg through vigorously, Akii-Bua finds that the foot of the lead leg contacts the ground slightly in front of the center of gravity. The theoretical advantage here would have been optimal if the foot had contacted the ground slightly behind the center of gravity. Here, Akii-Bua's forward upper body pitch helps to minimize any disadvantages, especially since this is 400m. hurdles and not 110m.

Figure 9 In this picture Akii-Bua has completely swung into the next stride. The driving right foot is perfectly stable with the heel almost touching the ground. This is a very strong position which completes the fast "leg pivot" that follows hurdle clearance to get the hurdler into the next stride without wasting time.

Figure 9 is an interesting picture. The knee of the driving leg is flexed and, with the lowering of the hips, the center of gravity is lowered. But more than those superficial mechanical details, what is happening here is that he is preventing an overemphasized vertical thrust which is dysfunctional in an event where success depends on horizontal speed. The flexed knee allows the hips time to rotate forward and to obtain a more effective drive. The trunk lean is perfectly advantageous. His arms are pretty well disposed and his shoulders are square to the direction of run. Idiosyncratically, the height of his head is on the excessive side, but he looks perfectly poised and smooth.

Figures 8-9 show positions which are crucial to many hurdlers. The trunk position from the first contact with the ground immediately after hurdle clearance until the trail leg is pulled through and swung into the next stride is vital. A premature opening up of the trunk hurries the trail leg. Consequently the hurdler hits the hurdle with his ankle or foot, the landing is unstable, and the first stride is short. In addition, the absorption of reactions by a low trunk at landing is impaired.

Figure 10 This picture shows a normal sprinting action. There seems to be a great deal of flexibility in the right ankle in its plantar flexion. The knee of the right leg is fully extended in the drive. Here you can see a combination of fast high leading knee action, forward lean, and powerful thrust from the driving foot, all of which give speed to the center of gravity in a forward direction.

Note: Before writing the preceding analysis of Akii-Bua's hurdling technique, I wrote down five basic points which I consider essential for a good hurdler to master. These are:

    (a) Correct take-off distance. This could not be measured in the picture, but Figure 2 gives us an idea of an effective take-off distance and an excellent drive action.

    (b) Forward rotation of the trunk at take off. This is easy to see from Figures 1-2.

    (c) Fast leading leg action combined with vigorous opposite arm action. This is difficult to extract from still photographs.

    (d) Long, low, drive from the take-off leg. This, of course, depends on the athlete's leg length, his hip mobility, and on the height of the hurdles. Akii-Bua's head level in the pictures analyzed did not indicate that his drive across the hurdles was a high one.

    (e) A good body dip. This, of course, Akii-Bua has, considering that he is *only* an intermediate hurdler.

As Ken Doherty has emphasized, the best time in hurdling ''is a resultant of maximum speed-skill-stamina.'' This was certainly true of Akii-Bua's world record run.

12

THE WOMEN'S HURDLES

Athlete: **Annelie Ehrhardt,** *East Germany*

Olympic Competition:
    100m. Hurdles   1972   1st   12.6 (Olympic Record)

Author: **Pierre Tissot van Patot** is a member of the editorial staff of the Netherland National Athletics Union magazine, *De Atletiek Wereld*, and is responsible for the coaching bulletin which accompanies that periodical. He is the official cinematographer of the K.N.A.U., for which he prepares instructional films, slow-motion loop films, and still-photo sequences with commentaries. He is a former club coach specializing in the coaching of the women's events; co-author of a series of texts on track and field; and a Member-of-Merit of the Netherlands Amateur Athletics Coaches Association, which he helped found in 1957.

In the women's 100m. hurdles race the stride pattern over the repeated distance cycle of 27 feet 10 inches (8.50 m.) might be put as follows, beginning with the first stride after clearing the hurdle: 4 feet 11 inches—6 feet 9 inches—6 feet 5 inches—9 feet 10 inches (150—205—195—300 cm.). The last mentioned distance, being the hurdle stride, is made up of an attack distance of 6 feet 9 inches (205 cm.) in front of the 2 feet 9 inches (84 cm.) hurdle and a landing distance of 3 feet 1 inch (95 cm.) behind it. As the average stride length of a woman sprinter amounts to about 6 feet 7 inches (200 cm.), the stride across the hurdle is obviously much longer. Several reasons are responsible for this big difference, although it is generally accepted that the hurdle clearance has to resemble a sprinting stride as much as possible. But first, the body's center of gravity has to be raised somewhat to negotiate the obstacle. Second, distance is needed to bring the lead leg above hurdle height at great speed. Third, both legs have to be raised much more than in running. And fourth, great speed and long take-off distance permit a more horizontal drive at the hurdle. Nevertheless, in spite of the long 9 feet 10 inch (300 cm.) stride, the hurdle clearance should be accomplished as fast as possible, to minimize the inevitable loss in time and speed. For a fast hurdle clearance leads to a rapid landing, a fast getaway, and a suitable first sprinting stride.

In respect to a fast hurdle clearance, Olympic Champion Annelie Ehrhardt excels as one of the best, if not the best, of the top women

Figure 1   Figure 2   Figure 3

hurdlers in the world. The photo sequence shows a hurdle stride of Eh-rhardt in her 100m. hurdles heat. Obviously, a photo sequence can not show speed nor rhythm, but an experienced observer can detect the smooth flow of movements or hesitations or breaks, and (more easily) right or wrong body positions.

Figures 1-2 show Ehrhardt's take off at about 6 feet 7 inches (2.0 m.) in front of the hurdle. Here the body forward lean, which is rarely very pronounced in the women's event, is just beginning. Starting this forward lean too early is a fault. In Figures 3-5 the trunk inclines gradually more and more as the hurdler is approaching and passing above the obstacle. However, it is noticed that Ehrhardt never dives sharply, but on the contrary, she uses even less body lean than do most women hurdlers.

The advantage of only little body lean is that it causes less deviation from normal sprint running technique and, generally, prevents unnecessary movements. But, the disadvantages of too little forward lean of the trunk are many and sometimes serious. The body's center of gravity will rise more, forcing the hurdler to direct her drive at the hurdle in more of an upwards direction. The swing of the leading leg will not be assisted by the indirect rotation provoked by and contrary to the downward rotation of the diving upper body (Figures 2-3). In crossing the hurdle the hip joint will be in an unfavorable position for an easy pulling through of the trailing take-off leg (Figures 5-7). When the trailing leg is rotating sideways to the front of the hip, this action will generate a contrary rotation of

Figure 4   Figure 5

the trunk, but if there is a good forward lean the angle of trunk rotation will be much smaller (Figures 6-7). Later on, in the landing phase beyond the hurdle (Figures 6-8), too little forward lean causes little straightening action of the trunk, which in turn will not provoke much extra indirect rotation for accelerating the downward movement of the landing leg. Also, it will be difficult to get the center of gravity vertically above the landing point (Figure 8).

However, it seems that Annelie Ehrhardt avoids the dangers mentioned, in spite of her relatively little trunk lean even for the low 2 feet 9 inch (84 cm.) hurdles. Moreover, she excels in bringing her trailing leg extremely fast and without hesitation over the hurdle. This movement is carried out late after take off, but when started it goes very fast and without hesitating above the hurdle (Figure 5-7). This hesitation is a common fault even with good hurdlers; it originates from the rather long hurdle stride.

A technically sound hurdle crossing will lead to a well-poised landing position beyond the hurdle and a smooth, unbroken change-over into the following first sprint-stride (Figures 7-9). The foot contacts the ground on the ball of the foot, the heel never drops down to the ground, the time being too short for a complete flattening and unwinding movement of the foot.

It is interesting to observe another two special points in Ehrhardt's hurdle technique, seemingly of not much importance but refinements that

Figure 6   Figure 7

may sometimes be of great individual help.

The first point is a rapid straightening of the swinging lead leg in approaching the hurdle (Figure 3). This is caused by a rapid whipping or kicking movement in the swing of this leg, which straightens the knee joint for a very short moment, just caught by the camera. Several top hurdlers like to use this leg-whipping, as they feel that the sharp stretching of the muscles at the back of the thigh provokes a reflexive contraction of these muscles, which aids in bringing the lead leg more rapidly over the hurdle and down to the ground.

The second point refers to the backward stretching of the arm on the lead leg side (Figures 1-4). The straightening of the elbow starts during the take off (Figures 1-2). The purpose of this seems to be to aid the just mentioned leading leg whip, according to the law of contrary movement and, perhaps most importantly, as a contrary movement which balances and aids the rapid forward pulling of the trailing leg (Figures 5-8).

A last remark, more of general importance, refers to the rather high clearance of the hurdles that can be observed with most women hurdlers, and Annelie Ehrhardt is no exception in this respect (Figure 5). Obviously, the clearance margin will depend somewhat upon the leg length in proportion to the hurdle height of 2 feet 9 inches (84 cm.). Annelie Ehrhardt is of average body height compared to other top women hurdlers. For the 20 competitors at the 1971 European Championships in Helsinki, the mean height was 5 feet 6¼ inches (168.4 cm.) and the mean

Figure 8   **Figure 9**

weight 128 pounds (58.15 kg.) with a maximum of 5 feet 8¾ inches (175 cm.), 141 pounds (64 kg.) and a minimum of 5 feet 3 inches (160 cm.), 110 pounds (50 kg.). Annelie Ehrhardt is 5 feet 5¼ inches (166 cm.), 128 pounds (58 kg.). In conclusion, it can be said that present-day women hurdlers could master very well a somewhat higher hurdle of say 3 feet (91 cm.).

13

THE 4 × 100m. RELAY EXCHANGE

Athletes: **Gerald Tinker to Eddie Hart,** *U.S.A.*

Olympic Competition:
    4 x 100m. Relay   1972   1st   38.2 (World Record)

Author: **John LeMasurier**, Principal National Coach for Great Britain, is another outstanding British coach of track and field. Coach of British Olympic teams (1960, 1964, 1968, 1972), English European Championships (1958, 1962, 1969, 1971), and Commonwealth Games teams (1954, 1966), he has also served as Coach of the European team vs. the Americas (1967) and Coach of the British Commonwealth team vs. U.S.A. and U.S.S.R. (1969). He is the author of seven books on track and field.

The photograph shows the final U.S. exchange from Gerald Tinker to anchor man Eddie Hart in the sprint relay at the Munich Olympics. The quartet, which had been led off by Larry Black and Robert Taylor, ran 38.19 seconds to win the final and to equal the world record set by C. Greene, M. Pender, R. Smith, and J. Hines four years previously in the thin air of Mexico City.

Twenty-seven national teams took part in the relay in Munich. The majority used an upsweep method of passing the baton with the lead-off runner carrying the baton in the right hand, No. 2 in the left, No. 3 right and No. 4 left (i.e. an alternate pass method). The U.S. team was one of the exceptions; Eddie Hart received the baton in his right hand from Gerald Tinker.

Whatever method is adopted, the most important factor is that the baton should be passed at speed. The speed of the outgoing runner must blend with that of the incoming runner. The passing zone is 20 meters in length, but the outgoing runner is permitted an extra 10 meters in which to accelerate before taking the baton. This area is frequently known as the accelerating zone.

Outgoing runners must standardize their starting method using an efficient standing start, a crouch, or a semicrouch position. A check mark placed back from the outgoing runner's start point can only be determined after practice under racing conditions. For sprinters of international class the check mark measurement is in the region of 30 "pigeon" steps (foot lengths) and should be clearly visible.

As soon as the incoming runner's hips cross the check mark the outgoing runner must accelerate away. During the initial period of acceleration the sprinter must use his arms vigorously and only place the receiving hand in position when he hears the call "Hand" from his incoming partner. Ideally the call should come in the second part of the take-over zone with the exchange taking place safely, smoothly and with baton speed maintained 3-4 yards from the far restraining line of the zone.

Even with such great sprinters as Black, Taylor, Tinker and Hart, to run 38.2 seconds calls for most efficient passing. In Munich the U.S. Quartet excelled themselves despite what some coaches would describe as an old-fashioned method.

The 4 x 100m. Relay Exchange

Photo: Ed Lacey
Track and Field News

14

THE 4 × 400m. RELAY EXCHANGE

Athletes: **Robert Ouko to Julius Sang,** *Kenya*

Olympic Competition:
    4 x 400m. Relay 1972   1st   2:59.8

Author: **John Velzian** is Head of the Sports Department at The University of Nairobi, Kenya. He coached track and field in Britain and Pakistan before moving to Kenya, where he was National Coach from 1964 to 1968.

Certainly one of the most exciting track events for me to watch, and an equally exciting one to coach, is the 4 x 400m. relay. Much of the appeal lies in the difficulty of attempting to assess the relative strength of each competing team. The method most often used is to add together the season's best 400m. time for each individual athlete—a method that has made past Kenyan 1600m. relay teams the most underestimated of all their track potential. Take for example their team in the Mexico Olympics. Not a single Kenyan figured in a world ranking list of the top thirty 400m. athletes, and in the 400m. event in Mexico only one of their team reached as far as 6th place in a semifinal. Who, on the strength of these performances, would have had the audacity to suggest that they would survive even the first round of the 4 x 400m. relay, let alone equal the existing world record and lose the gold medal only to the greatest team of 400m. athletes ever to set foot on a track?

The reason for this unpredictability of the Kenyans in the relay is not difficult to find. Running the individual event in lanes requires a precise knowledge of pace judgment gained from countless races in every lane against all sorts of opposition, experience which few Kenyans in the past were able to acquire. In the relay, however, a far more natural form of man-to-man race develops for almost three-quarters of the event. A good example of how this is better suited to the unsophisticated attitude to running which some Kenyans have is seen in the case of Daniel Rudisha in Mexico. Eliminated in the second round of the 400m. event in a time of only 47.6, he chased home the great Lee Evans in the final leg of the relay in a time of 44.4 seconds!

The story in Munich was somewhat different for a number of reasons. In Sang and Asati the Kenyans now had two world-class 400m. athletes, Sang being one of the only two non-Americans in the world's top-ranked dozen and a half. Both the other two Kenyans were also highly experienced athletes, providing a team of the same four individuals who had gained the gold medal in the Commonwealth Games in 1970. This, then, was not only far more talented and experienced than any previous Kenyan team, it was also one which had been selected only after a great deal of close competition for a place. For whereas in the past there had always been a difficulty of who to add to the 400m. specialists to make up the number, at the time of Munich there was an abundance of high-class single-lap athletes. One has only to consider the position of Julius Sang

4 x 400m.

Photo: Don Chadez
Track and Field News

and Robert Ouko to appreciate this. Both had been studying at North Carolina Central in the U.S.A., during which time Sang had notched a victory over Lee Evans and Vince Mathews in a time of 45.3 despite heavy weather conditions, and Ouko still had a sub-46.0 to his credit, times one would have thought good enough to secure a place at least in the relay squad if not in the individual event as well. But the Kenyans have no respect for reputations, especially those gained overseas on first-class tracks against world-class opposition, and for the first few track meets after these two returned home to establish their place in the Munich team it was by no means certain that they would be going to the Olympics at all. In the first of the two final Olympic Trials Sang could manage nothing better than a fourth place in a 400m. in which the fastest Kenyan was not competing. With three others already qualified for Munich in this event his position was doubtful, a fact that was further underlined in the Final Olympic Trials when he finished last. Ouko likewise had a stormy passage, failing hopelessly in the 400m. races and only just making the final of the 800m. as the faster loser. With no fewer than five other Kenyans already qualified in this he had to produce his Commonwealth gold medal winning time of 1:46.0 to make sure of his ticket.

Considering the failure of these two athletes over the 400m. how then does the photograph on page 000 come to show Ouko handing over to Sang for the final leg of the 4 x 400m. relay in Munich? For both athletes this story hinges around William Koskei, Kenya's 400m. intermediate hurdler who was heading a world ranking list in this event when Sang and Ouko were striving for their places in the team. Some sound performances over the 400m. well inside the qualifying standard and also earned him a probable place in the relay team. Wisely he decided to tackle only the hurdles and the relay in Munich and this gave Sang a place in the 400m. on the strength of his performances in the United States. The remainder of Sang's story is clearly written in the Munich results. A return to form saw him run superb races throughout to finish with a bronze behind Vince Mathews and Wayne Collet after John Smith had pulled up lame shortly after leaving his blocks. Needless to say this assured Sang of his place in the relay. But Koskei's dreams of medals were to disappear when a bad bout of malaria left him so physically weak and disturbed by his condition that he was eliminated in the first round of the 400m. hurdles, and Ouko therefore had to step in to replace him in the relay.

Changes in the composition of a relay squad must always be expected in Games like the Olympics. The long period of preparation and competition that have led up to the games, and the actual games once they have begun, will take their toll in terms of illness and injury and loss of form, and this will effect not only the final selection of a team, but also the order in which they will run. Of course, if the team has selected itself, as in the ruthlessly fierce arena of the United States Olympic Trials, and consists of the four fastest 400m. athletes in the world with probably the next six fastest also from the U.S.A., as was the case both at Mexico and Munich, it makes no difference whether they are run in ascending or descending order of merit or no order at all, barring accident they must take home the gold as they have done in every Olympic competition prior to Munich except three.

But for lesser teams whose athletes have been scattered throughout the heats of their respective individual events and who may also have to fill a place with a nonspecialist 400m. man, both the composition of the team and its order of running may well have to be left till a fairly late hour. Fortunately this is possible since baton hand-overs do not require the same degree of skill between two specific individuals as does the shorter sprint relay. This is not to say it is unimportant, for there can never be a substitute for perfection in an event in which hundredths of a second can count at the finish; it merely recognizes that a good hand-over requires more that the outgoing runner be able to read the speed and condition of his tiring team mate than time spent in practice.

So much then for the factors that influenced the final selection of the four Kenyans who ran the 4 x 400m. relay in Munich. What can we say about their actual order of running? The Kenyans ran their team in the order of Asati, Nyamau, Ouko and Sang in both the heats and the final. As such it meant that their fastest athlete would finish, the second fastest would start, the third fastest would take the third leg, and the slowest the second leg. Remembering that an error in seeding had drawn the Americans and the Kenyans in the same heat, this seemed as good an order as any, for, in both the heat and the final the Kenyans would have had the faster Americans out front to pull against. But when the Americans failed to appear for the heat it became immediately apparent that the Kenyans would now be faced with two very different races, a heat which they would probably win from out front all the way and a final which would now be very much tighter and which would possibly require a change in running order if they were to convert their certain silver with the Americans in the race to a certain gold without them.

In the heats, Sang ran a very easy and confident anchor leg to allow the British to pull up and gain a narrow verdict in the same time of 3:01.3.

Although this fine run by the British suggested that they would be in with a chance for a medal, there was little doubt that this would have to be either silver or bronze. Poland and Finland qualified well in their heat, the former significantly from out front all the way, but again there seemed little threat to the gold. Clearly this would still come from the West Germans, since they also had two 400m. finalists, but they had drawn the easiest of the three heats and in winning it comfortably in a time that was a full 2 seconds slower than the Kenyans gave no indication of just how great this threat would be. What was obvious, however, was that with Sang in superb form to run the anchor leg for Kenya the only hope the West Germans would have of the gold would be to be well in the lead at this stage. An indication that they were perhaps thinking along these lines was seen in their heat when they ran Schloeske, their fastest athlete, on the second leg. Consequently I would have argued a change in the running order of the Kenyans in the following way:

If Asati were to lead off he would be expected to put the Kenyans ahead since he would be the fastest athlete on this leg. But to hand over to Nyamau, the slowest of the Kenyans, for the second leg, would be doing exactly what the West Germans would wish for, since it would give the faster Schloeske someone to pull against and then pile on the pressure to open up as big a lead as possible. If Koehler could hold this lead against Ouko the Kenyans could possibly be in trouble. Knowing that the Kenyans invariably run faster relay legs when chasing than when leading, the obvious solution to this problem would lie in not putting the Kenyans in the lead until they could be certain of holding it right through to the finishing tape. This would rule out running either Asati or Sang for the first leg, leaving a choice of Nyamau or Ouko. But whereas Nyamau was a specialist 400m. athlete capable of running a sound race from any lane, Ouko had run few 400m. races in lanes that year and it would be unwise to give him this responsibility. Nyamau would therefore have to lead off. It would be too much to expect that he would put the Kenyans ahead, but he certainly would not have left them very far down. Assuming that Sang would still run the anchor leg, this would leave Ouko and Asati to run the two middle legs. If Ouko were to take over we could expect the West Germans to go farther ahead, but since it would now be Scholeske who would have to run out front whilst Ouko would have others to pull against, the West German lead would be minimized. Running in this order we could expect the Kenyans to be down at the half way stage, but with Asati and Sang, the two fastest athletes in the entire race, to take the final 800m. I would have been very confident of the end result. However, there was a further possible way of tackling this which involved nothing more than a reversal of the running order of the first two athletes. As already discussed, we could expect Schloeske to cut back any lead which Asati would give Nyamau if the Kenyans ran their team in the same order in the final as they had done in the heats. But if Nyamau were to lead off and hand over to Asati, who would be slightly down but would have the faster of the Germans out front, I would have expected a very fast leg from Asati to prevent any possibility of the West Germans opening up a decisive lead. Nyamau, Asati, Ouko and Sang would therefore have been my running order for the Kenyans in the final.

This may well seem like being wise after the event, but as just explained, so much of the race as it was eventually run had been predictable. The Kenyans made no change in their running order for the final and Asati led off to put his team ahead, although not as dramatically as in Mexico when he outran Vince Mathews, Munich's 400m. gold medalist, in the race in which the Americans set up the 4 x 400m. world record that exists today. At the end of the first leg the position was: 1. Kenya (45.3) 2. West Germany (45.8) 3. Poland (46.0), 4. Sweden (46.0), 5. France (46.2), 6. Great Britain (46.3) and 7. and 8. Finland and Trinidad (46.7).

Nyamau was therefore set up for Schloeske, who slid by on the inside just before the end of the back straight and then surged on to record a fine 44.5 and put the West Germans some seven yards ahead of the Kenyans. The danger of putting the slowest of the Kenyans out front at this stage was further seen when Balachowski of Poland also used Nyamau to pull against and cut back the lead, overtaking him in the home straight to put Poland in second place. Not only that, but six of the seven athletes who had been behind Nyamau when he went into the lead were able to record faster times on this leg, and both Velasquez of France and Pascoe of Britain were able to bring their teams up just behind the Kenyans. Position at the end of the second leg: 1. West Germany (1:30.3), 2. Poland (1:31.0), 3. Kenya (1:31.1), 4. France (1:31.2), 5. Great Britain (1:31.4), 6. Sweden (1:31.5), 7. Finland (1:31.8) and 8. Trinidad (1:32.7).

For the third leg everything for the West Germans depended upon Köhler being able to hold this lead. But once again we were to see the disadvantage that the front runner has in this relay, for all seven athletes were able to record faster times than Kohler. Ouko put the Kenyans into second place but again lost this position to Jaremski of Poland, while Hemery put Great Britain ahead of France only to lose this advantage at the take-over. So tense was the race at this stage that superb legs by

Joseph of Trinidad (44.5) and Karttunen of Finland (44.8) went un-
noticed. Position at the end of the third leg: 1. West Germany (2:15.9), 2.
Poland (2:16.2), 3. Kenya (2:16.3), 4. France (2:16.4), 5. Great Britain
(2:16.4), 6. Finland (2:16.6), 7. Sweden (2:16.8) and 8. Trinidad
(2:17.2).

Although the Kenyans had pulled back some of the West German
lead they were still a clear four yards down when Sang took over for the
final leg. Honz blasted off an unbelievably fast 20.1 for the first 200m. to
give the West Germans a clear look at the gold medal, and Badenski of
Poland was not far behind with a 20.3. But both of these great European
athletes were to pay dearly for their overenthusiastic start. Sang moved
with almost effortless ease to flash past Badenski on the final bend and
then attack the now failing Honz who was clearly in trouble. The roaring
partisan crowd sensed the danger and by the time Sang drew level with
Honz some 80 yards from home the stadium was almost hushed. At
almost the same time Jenkins of Great Britain (44.1) moved past
Badenski and then slowly overhauled Honz, taking him some 40 yards
from the finish to give Great Britain the silver. But the bronze medal was
not determined till right on the finishing line when Honz went sprawling
to leave his team in the miserable position of fourth, and allow Carette,
who had run a remarkable 44.3, to squeeze by and give France an unex-
pected medal. Badenski only just managed to put Poland into fifth place
and Finland, Sweden and Trinidad brought up the rear.

1. Kenya	—Charles Asati 45.3, Hezekiah Nyamau 45.8, Robert Ouko 45.2, Julius Sang 43.5	2:59.83
2. Great Britain	—Martin Reynolds 46.3, Alan Pascoe 45.1 David Hemery 45.0, David Jenkins 44.1	3:00.46
3. France	—Gilles Bertould 46.2, Daniel Vélasquez 45.0, Francis Kerbiriou 45.2, Jacques Carette 44.3	3:00.65
4. West Germany	—Bernd Herrmann 45.8, H-Rüdiger Schlöske 44.5, Hermann Köhler 45.6, Karl Honz 45.0	3:00.88
5. Poland	—Jan Werner 46.0, Jan Balachowski 45.0, Zbigniew Jaremski 45.2, Andrzej Badénski 44.9	3:01.05
6. Finland	—Stig Lönnqvist 46.7, Ari Salin 45.1 Ossi Karttunen 44.8, Markku Kukkoaho 44.5	3:01.12
7. Sweden	—Eric Carlgren 46.0, Anders Faager 45.5, Kenth Ohman 45.3, Ulf Rönner 45.8	3:02.57
8. Trinidad & Tobago	—Arthur Cooper 46.7, Pat Marshall 46.0 Charles Joseph 44.5, Ed Roberts 46.4	3:03.60

Clearly this race belonged to Sang. Had he run a 44.6, a sound leg of a relay by any standards, the Kenyans would have received no medal at all. Instead he ran a full 1.1 second faster than this for the fastest leg ever of a 1600m. relay at sea level, and one which has been bettered only once when Ron Freeman ran a 43.2 in the more favorable rarified atmosphere of Mexico City as his contribution to a great 4 x 400m. world record. Yet it is interesting to note that despite this amazing leg by Sang the final time of 2:59.8 for the Kenyans was still slower than that of their far less-talented team in Mexico. No doubt the lack of altitude and the absence of the Americans had something to do with this, but so also I feel did the order in which the Kenyans ran their team.

There will, of course, always be arguments such as what could, would or should have happened had this been that, but in the final analysis the only argument that counts is what is written in the record book. In the Official Report of the 1972 Munich Olympic Games this shows clearly that it was an undisputed gold medal for the Kenyans —even if it was somewhat tarnished by the forced withdrawal of the American team.

15

THE WALKS

Athletes:	1972 Olympic Competition	
	20 km	50 km
#301 Paul Nihill, *Great Britain*	6th	9th
#326 Peter Frenkel, *East Germany*	1st (1:26:42:4— Olympic Record)	—
#372 Bernd Kannenberg, *West Germany*	dnf	1st (3:56:11.6— Olympic Record)
#537 Vittorio Visini, *Italy*	8th	7th

Author: **Chris McCarthy** won national championships in the 40km. and 50km. walks (1963), the 35km., 40km. and 50km. walks (1964), and represented the U.S.A. in the 50 km. walk at the 1964 Olympic Games. He is a former editor of *Race Walker*.

This picture taken shortly after the start of the 20km. walk at the Munich Olympic Games shows the leaders bunched together as they round the first turn prior to leaving the stadium. Note that the leader, Nihill (#301), is proceeding with his head bent much too low. In walking as in running, this tends to restrict the inflow of air to the lungs. Much better in this regard is the eventual winner, Frenkel (#326) immediately behind him. Kannenberg (#372), was also a bit marginal when this photo was taken.

Equally noteworthy in this photo is the lateral thrust of Nihill's left hip. To some extent this phenomenon is exhibited by all race walkers and only an excess can be avoided. Immediately after his heel lands, the walker proceeds to straighten the knee of his supporting leg, and using his arms to gain added thrust (as well as to maintain his balance) he evacuates the trailing leg by pivoting around on his hip. Inevitably this results in a lateral displacement of the pelvic girdle. Coaches should tak care that the walker does not exhibit a wiggly, side-to-side motion. If we were to imagine a pole thrust down through the center of the hip girdle the walker would pivot his hips about that pole; but the pole itself would not move from side to side.

Note further the dip of Nihill's left shoulder. Then notice how his left hip is elevated. Follow the elastic of his shorts and observe how it slopes downward to the left. Just as some lateral displacement of the hips is inevitable, some vertical displacement of the hips and shoulders is also inevitable. Again it is a matter of degree and only an excess can be avoided. The walker does not merely rotate his hips in a horizontal plane. If our imaginary pole were now placed through our walker's hips parallel to the ground, we would find that it does not only rotate back and forth but it also moves up and down, much like the paddle of a kayak. At the same time the shoulders follow a similar, but opposite motion. As the left hip goes up, the left shoulder goes down. When done to excess the result is a compression or strain on the body. A further result is that the walker tends to ride back on his hips resulting in an exaggerated locking of the knee of the supporting leg. At 20 km. such exaggerated locking can be painful. At 50 km. it can be fatal.

As the walker approaches the double contact phase (the instant at which both feet will be on the ground simultaneously) the rotation of his hips will be at the maximum. If the walker did not rotate his hips, his stride would be greatly shortened. By merely swinging his hips around he can gain a couple of extra inches of stride length without the extra (and self-defeating) effort of stretching out. But again, how much is too much?

20km. Walk

Photo: Don Chadez

Too much is literally when the walker starts to tear himself apart. Many of the injuries of race-walking are connected with overtwisting of the hips. A coach can often detect this simply by listening. A walker with crepe soles shoes who is overtwisting his hips makes a squish-squish sound. If he is walking on a dirt track he leaves a small hole. The soles of his shoes will develop gouges between the ball of the foot and the toe.

Overtwisting of the hips, especially when coupled with overstretching of the legs, can easily lead to loss of contact with the ground. Note the marginal contact of Frenkel, the walker immediately behind Nihill. The toe of his trailing leg is about to break contact with the ground, yet the heel of his foward foot has not yet landed. A judge cannot, of course, actually observe this. Only a camera can. But what a judge can detect is that such a walker appears to be very high. He appears to be floating, or close to it. With good firm contact there is considerable overlap during the double contact phase. For example, Visini (#537), is approaching the double contact phase with the ball of his trailing foot still on the ground. A judge observing this would detect that Visini is lower down and thus safer than Frenkel, who is risking disqualification.

In addition to the rule requiring that the walker maintain continuous contact with the ground, race-walking further requires that the leg must be straightened at the knee for at least an instant during the period of each stride. Unfortunately, until recently the rules did not specify at which instant the leg had to be straightened and this led to considerable controversy. The "creepers" (those who preceeded on bent knees) used to argue that their legs would straighten either as they landed or as they left. Extensive study of slow motion films, however, revealed that if the walker does not have his leg straightened by the time the traveling leg passes the supporting leg, he will usually not straighten it at all. The only exception is when the creeper is really stretching out, as in a sprint for the tape or when passing, or when engaged in other such maneuvers. But these are the very times when the walker is in most danger of losing contact with the ground.

Prior to the Munich Olympics the I.A.A.F. rules were amended to specify that the supporting leg must be straightened at the knee at the instant during which the traveling leg passes by. Returning again to our photo, notice the exemplary manner in which Nihill is complying with this rule. Note too that Kannenberg has his supporting leg actually bowed back (locked). To some extent this is a function of the photo itself. Immediately after the traveling leg passes the supporting leg, the walker is said to be entering the anterior supporting phase. During the early part of the anterior supporting phase the locking of the leg reaches its maximum (Kannenberg); during the later part of the anterior supporting phase the supporting leg begins to break at the knee (Visini).

Coaches and judges need not worry about whether their athletes have their knees straightened at the instant the traveling leg passes by. As with loss of contact it happens so quickly that direct observation is not always possible. It is sufficient to know that if the walker has straightened at all, he will have straightened by that time. If he hasn't straightened, that is, if he is creeping, then the observable effect will be a sit-down type of walking, somewhat akin to the old Groucho Marx crawl. As long as you can see the more pronounced straightening and/or locking of the early anterior supporting phase you can be sure your athlete is complying. Photo analysis has shown this to be so.

In passing, and by way of summary, it might be well to throw in a caveat. In a very fundamental way race-walking is not a democratic sport. At least not in the way that running is. Almost anybody can run, or at least jog. But only those who are capable of fully straightening their legs will be able to compete in race-walking. Fortunately there are exercises which will help the creeper comply. Particularly valuable is the hurdler's exercise, using both hands for pressure on the forward knee. Deliberate overlocking at low speeds also helps, especially if a short stick is held between the small of the back and the crook of the arms while walking. The effect of this is to force the legs to straighten.

PART TWO
The Jumping Events

16

FUNDAMENTAL MECHANICS
OF JUMPING

Author: **Jim Hay** is an Associate Professor of Physical Education at the University of Iowa. A former pole vaulter, he has served as coach of the New Zealand team at the Pacific Conference Games, (1969) and as President of the New Zealand Amateur Athletic Coaches' Association (1970). He has conducted extensive research into the mechanics of the jumping events over the past ten years, has instructed at numerous clinics both in the U.S. and in New Zealand, and has written a comprehensive text entitled *The Biomechanics of Sports Techniques* (Prentice-Hall, Inc., 1973).

When analyzing techniques in the jumping events it is customary to consider the actions performed by the athlete in the order in which they occur. Thus, most analyses deal with the approach run, the preparation for take off (the "coast" or "gather" in the long, triple and high jumps and the plant in the pole vault), the take off, the flight and the landing, in that order. While this sequential approach to the analysis of the jumping events is simple and straightforward, it all too frequently obscures the basic mechanical relationships governing the quality of performance. For this reason the method perferred here is one which involves three simple steps:

(1) the subdivision of the athlete's objective (distance in the horizontal jumps and height in the vertical ones) into a number of smaller parts,

(2) identification of the mechanical factors that influence or determine the magnitude of each of these parts, and

(3) discussion of the techniques needed to maximize (or optimize) each of these mechanical factors during the performance of the event.

Note: In the mechanical analyses which follow, steps (2) and (3) proceed simultaneously.

LONG JUMP

Assuming that he abides by all the rules governing the event and that he does not touch the ground behind the line of his heels when he lands, the distance with which a long jumper is credited may be thought of as being the sum of (1) the horizontal distance which his center of gravity is in front of the scratch-line (i.e. the front edge of the board) at take off, (2) the horizontal distance which his center of gravity travels while he is air-borne and (3) the horizontal distance which his heels are in front of his center of gravity at the moment they break the sand. These three distances—the take-off distance (L_1), the flight distance (L_2), and the landing distance (L_3)—are shown in Figure 1.

The take-off distance (positive, zero, or negative depending on whether the jumper's center of gravity is in front, directly above, or behind the scratch-line at take off) depends mainly on the "accuracy" of the run-up. If the jumper arrives at the board with the toes of his take-off foot close to the scratch-line (on the legal side!) his take-off distance is likely to act in his favor to the extent of perhaps 6-10 inches (15-25 cm.). However, if his run-up is not that "accurate" and he takes off some distance behind the board, his take-off distance will be negative. Under these circumstances the jumper operates under a self-imposed handicap—he must actually jump some distance in order to bring himself level with the scratch-line.

Figure 1

The take-off distance is also influenced to some extent by the physique of the athlete (tall, long-limbed athletes may obtain greater take-off distances than those less endowed) and by his body position at the moment of take off.

The flight distance (which, incidentally, contributes some 85 to 90 percent of the total distance in good jumping) depends primarily on the nature of the take off—a fact which accounts for the often-heard remark, "I could tell it was going to be a good one the moment I left the board." Like the center of gravity of any other projectile whose flight is not seriously influenced by air resistance, the center of gravity of a long jumper follows a parabolic path. The exact dimensions of this parabolic flight path are determined by the jumper's velocity at take off and, to a lesser extent, by the height of his center of gravity at take off. The jumper's velocity at take off (about 30 feet per second [9.1 m./sec] for a 26 foot [7.92 m.] jump) depends on the horizontal velocity he obtains from his run-up and on the vertical velocity he obtains by driving forcefully downward against the board. Because the jumper has a virtually unlimited time in which to build up horizontal velocity and only a split-second to acquire vertical velocity, it is the former of these two that makes by far the greater contribution to his velocity at take off. For this reason sheer sprinting speed is of critical importance in long jumping—a point that is well-illustrated by the fact that very few athletes with less than 9.6 seconds 100 yards speed have ever exceeded 26 feet (7.92 m.) in the long jump.

The angle of take off (which, strictly speaking, is included when one refers to the "velocity of take off") is also greatly influenced by the differences in the times which the athlete has available to generate horizontal and vertical velocities. Although the optimum angle of take off for a top-class jumper can be shown mathematically to be close to 45 degrees, in practice it is impossible for an athlete to attain such an angle unless he decreases his horizontal velocity markedly. While this slowing down gives the athlete more time to generate a vertical velocity near-equal to his horizontal velocity (something he'd need if he were to have a take-off angle approaching 45 degrees) anything he might gain from having a theoretically optimum angle of take off is far outweighed by the huge losses he incurs as a result of decreasing his take-off velocity. In practice, therefore, long jumpers try to get as much vertical velocity as they can with the least loss in horizontal velocity. This generally results in angles of take off in the order of 18 to 22 degrees.

The landing distance depends on the jumper's body position as he lands in the pit and on the movements he makes subsequently to avoid sitting back. The body position that the jumper adopts in preparation for landing is largely dictated by the nature of the rotation he acquired during the take off and by what he does about it during the flight. (It should be stressed here that since the flight path of the jumper's center of gravity cannot be altered by his actions in the air—a well-established scientific fact—such actions serve only to aid in putting the jumper's body in the best position for landing.)

Although it is possible to leave the board with either forward or backward rotation about an axis through the center of gravity (all in-the-air rotations take place about an axis through the center of gravity) or indeed with no rotation at all, in practice most long jumpers possess some forward rotation at the moment they become air-borne. And, since the amount of rotation (i.e. the angular momentum) which an athlete posses-ses at this time cannot be altered in flight (the so-called Conservation of Angular Momentum Principle) all he can do is to try to make sure that his body does not rotate so far that he is unable to get his feet well forward for the landing.

To understand how this may be accomplished it is first necessary to have a good understanding of the Conservation of Angular Momentum principle. The angular momentum that a rotating body possesses is equal to the product of two factors—one is a measure of how the mass of the body is distributed relative to the axis of rotation (the moment of inertia) and the other is the rate at which the body is rotating about that axis (the angular velocity). It is the angular momentum, this product of the mo-ment of inertia and the angular velocity, which remains constant through-out the air-borne phase of the jump. Now, if a jumper leaves the board with some forward rotation and then decreases his moment of inertia by assuming a tucked or piked position—as in the sail style of jump used by most beginners—his angular velocity is increased. (Because this is the only way that his angular momentum could possibly remain constant, the angular velocity increases when the moment of inertia is decreased and vice versa.) The net result is that the jumper's body generally rotates so far forward that he lands with his feet beneath, or almost beneath, his center of gravity. As a rule, therefore, jumpers who use the sail style only rarely achieve respectable landing distances.

Athletes who use the hang style are generally much more effective in controlling their forward rotation and ensuring an efficient landing. Once the jumper has left the board he sweeps his leading leg in a downward and backward direction. (In accord with Newton's law of reaction, this action produces a contrary upward and backward reaction of the athlete's trunk). Thus, as a result of the actions of the jumper's leading leg, the trunk is brought back to (and often slightly beyond) an erect position. In addition, since the athlete's body is near-fully extended as a result of these actions (and its moment of inertia is therefore almost as large as it can be), the athlete's forward angular velocity is reduced correspondingly. Exponents of the hitch-kick or "running-in-the-air" style employ basically the same methods as do those who use the hang style except that instead of sweeping the leading leg back and then, after some delay, bringing both legs forward for landing, they sweep each leg back alternately before finally bringing them together for the landing. In this way they are able to markedly increase the backward rotation of the trunk which such actions produce.

Once the jumper's heels have cut the sand, his main concern is to avoid falling back and thus lessening the distance of the jump. To this end, he allows his hip, knee and ankle joints to "collapse" (thereby decreasing his moment of inertia and increasing his angular velocity relative to an axis through his ankles) and, swings his arms forward (to give added forward momentum to his body).

The relationships between the distance jumped and the various factors which influence that distance are shown diagrammatically in Figure 2.

TRIPLE JUMP

For the purposes of analysis, the distance with which a triple jumper is credited may be subdivided in a manner similar to that already outlined with reference to the long jump. In this instance, however, there are three take-off distances, three flight distances and three landing distances which must be taken into account. Furthermore, since the length of the second and third phases in the sequence depend a great deal on what has taken place in the preceding phase or phases, the jumper is most unwise if he attempts to obtain the maximum distance of which he is capable in either of the first two phases. Instead he must strive for that combination of distances which will yield the greatest total for the three phases. In general this means keeping the first phase relatively low and short (i.e. compared with the maximum he could produce with just a single hop), the second phase near the best he can produce, and the third phase at the maximum possible under the circumstances.

HIGH JUMP

The height with which an athlete is credited in the high jump may be thought of as the sum of (1) the height of his center of gravity at take off, (2) the height which his center of gravity is lifted during the jump, and (3)

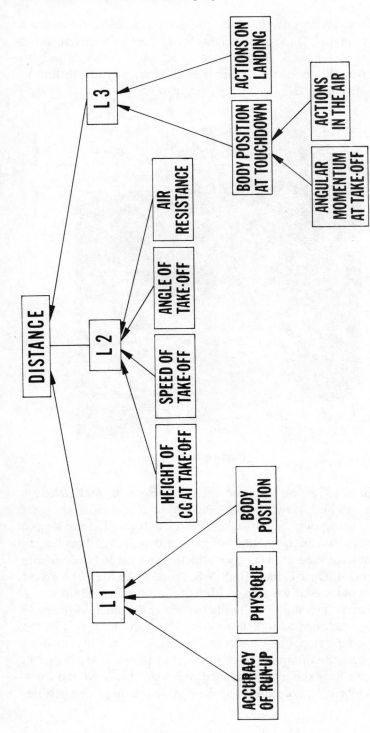

Figure 2

the difference between the height of the bar and the peak height attained by his center of gravity. These three heights are respectively designated as H_1, H_2, and H_3 in Figure 3. *Note:* Since an athlete's center of gravity must almost invariably be lifted higher than the bar in order for him to make a successful jump, H_3 is generally negative.

Figure 3

The height of the center of gravity at the moment the athlete leaves the ground depends on just two factors—his physique and his body position. From the standpoint of physique, the fact that tall, long-legged athletes invariably have higher centers of gravity than short, short-legged ones explains in large measure why such athletes have tended to dominate the event—Figure 4. (Juri Tarmak [U.S.S.R.] and Ulrike Meyfahrt [West Germany], the gold medal winners in Munich, are respectively 6 feet 4 inches and 6 feet ½ inch tall). While the particular demands of the style being used (e.g. the need to initiate rotation about the long axis of the body in the Fosbury flop) may make it impossible to achieve or even unwise to attempt, the optimum body position in terms of H_1 is one in which the jumper has both arms extended overhead, his head and trunk erect and "stretched," his leading leg straight and as high as possible,

Photo: Peter Francis

Figure 4

and his take-off leg fully extended at knee and ankle joints. The take-off position of former world-record holder, John Thomas (U.S.A.) is probably nearer to this optimum than that achieved by any other jumper to date (Figure 5).

The magnitude of H_2, the amount of lift the athlete gets, is governed simply by his vertical velocity at the moment he leaves the ground. This, in turn, is governed by (a) the vertical velocity of his center of gravity at the instant the heel of his take-off foot is planted prior to take off, and (b) the change in the vertical velocity of his center of gravity brought about during the take off. In other words, his vertical velocity at take off is equal to his vertical velocity at touchdown or foot plant, plus whatever change in vertical velocity he can effect during the take off.

The vertical velocity of the athlete's center of gravity at the moment the heel of his take-off foot is planted is determined by his actions during the last strides of his run-up. If he simply maintains a normal running action, his center of gravity follows a fairly smooth undulating path, moving downward and forward at the instant each foot is planted and then upward and forward as he is driven into the next stride. Such a method of

Figure 5

executing the last few strides of the run-up has the distinct disadvantage that, once the athlete has planted his take-off foot, he must first arrest the downward motion of his center of gravity before he can begin work on the critical task of propelling it upward into the air. In short, he must waste some of his effort to reverse the vertical direction in which his body is moving. To overcome this problem, most good jumpers modify their actions during the final stages of the run-up so that the last stride begins with the hip, knee and ankle joints of the supporting leg well flexed and the center of gravity low. From this position, the athlete drives his hips forward and upward and reaches his take-off foot forward so that, after a very short flight phase (as little as .01 second for some jumpers), the heel is planted *before the center of gravity begins to descend*. Thus, at the instant of touchdown, the athlete's center of gravity has either a zero or, perhaps, a small upward vertical velocity.

The extent to which an athlete can change his vertical velocity during the take off is governed by the product of the vertical forces he exerts and the time for which they act, i.e., by a quantity known as the vertical impulse. Although one's first inclination may be to suggest that the ath-

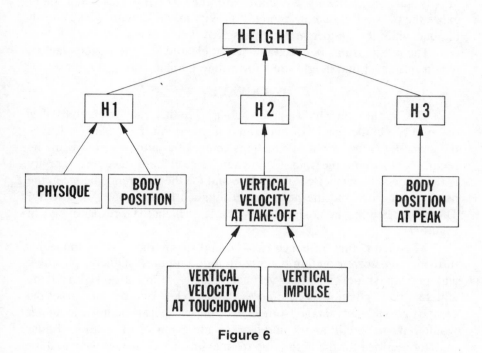

Figure 6

lete should therefore strive to increase both the magnitude of the vertical forces which he exerts against the ground and the time for which they act (and, thus, the time of take off), it has been shown repeatedly that the less time an athlete is in contact with the ground at take off, the higher he goes. For some reason, which has yet to be adequately explained, the magnitude of the vertical forces that an athlete exerts increase at a greater rate than the time of take off decreases. Thus a decrease in the time of take off is generally accompanied by increases in both the vertical impulse and the vertical velocity at take off.

The magnitude of H_3 (the height of the bar minus the peak height reached by the jumper's center of gravity) is governed mainly by the jumper's body position as he crosses the bar. If the jumper uses a simple scissors technique, his center of gravity may have to be lifted as much as 10-12 inches above the bar in order that he can effect a clearance $H_3 = $ —10-12 inches). With more advanced jumping techniques—eastern cut-off, western roll, straddle, and Fosbury flop—the magnitude of the difference between the height of the bar and the peak height of the center of gravity gets progressively less until, with the last two styles listed, there exists the possibility that the center of gravity might actually pass beneath the bar while the jumper himself passes over it.

The relationships between the height cleared and the various factors which influence that height are shown diagrammatically in Figure 6.

POLE VAULT

The height with which a pole vaulter is credited may be thought of as the sum of (1) the height of his center of gravity at the instant he leaves the ground, (2) the height to which his center of gravity is raised while he retains contact with the pole, (3) the height to which his center of gravity is raised once he has let go of the pole and (4) the difference between the height of the bar and the peak height attained by his center of gravity. These four heights are designated as H_1; H_2, H_3 and H_4, respectively, in Figure 7.

The factors that influence H_1, H_3, and H_4 are the same as those that influence the corresponding heights in high jumping—namely, physique and body position (H_1), the vertical velocity at release (H_3) and the athlete's body position as he crosses the bar (H_4). In order to extract the greatest possible advantage from each of these separate heights, a vaulter would have to be tall, and would have to adopt a take-off position similar to that described for the high jump (to maximize H_1); would have to have as high a vertical velocity as possible at the time he releases the pole (to maximize H_3); and, would have to use the most tightly-draped clearance position which would still permit him to clear the bar (to optimize H_4). In practice, however, a series of compromises is necessary because these conditions which serve to maximize one height often act to the detriment of the next. For example, to get a maximum value of H_1 a vaulter could attempt to use a lead leg action like that of high-jumper John Thomas (p. 128). Such an action, however, would make it extremely difficult for the vaulter to obtain the best results possible in the next phases of the vault. He might gain perhaps 1-2 inches (2.5-5.1 cm.) in H_1 (c.f. the more orthodox method of leaving the ground) only to lose perhaps 1-2 feet (30.5-61 cm.) in the value of H_2.

Of the four contributions to the height which the vaulter clears, the height which his center of gravity is raised while he is in contact with the

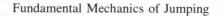

Figure 7

pole (H_2) is by far the most important—H_2 may contribute as much as 13 feet, 3.96m. (or 72%) in the case of an 18 feet (5.49 m.) vault.

While a complete analysis of the factors that influence the magnitude of H_2 requires a somewhat involved discussion of the interplay of energy between the vaulter and his pole, it is sufficient here to consider just three of the factors concerned—(a) the vaulter's velocity at take off, (b) the energy he has "stored" in the pole at that time, and (c) the work he does as the pole rises towards the vertical.

The vaulter's velocity at take off, determined by the speed of his approach and by the forces he exerts at take off, is important in that it influences the amount of pole-bend he obtains and, partly as a consequence, his ability to bring the pole to the vertical (or desired near-vertical) position required for completion of the vault. Because of this, the good vaulter tries to acquire as much forward speed in his run-up as he can control, to maintain it during the plant when there is a natural tendency to slow down and, finally, to exert forces at take off so that his body is propelled in the optimum direction. In vaulting with a metal pole (where pole-bend is generally not a significant factor) this optimum direction is approximately at right angles to the line of the pole—the direction which provides the best chance of the pole being brought to the required vertical (or near-vertical) release position. With a fiberglass pole, the need to bend the pole dictates that the vaulter direct his take off somewhat more horizontally than if he were using a metal pole. Thus, present-day vaulters take off at angles of 15-25 degrees, angles similar to those used by top-class long jumpers whose take off they purposely try to emulate.

The energy that a vaulter is able to "store" in a pole prior to take off—for any given pole, this may be thought of simply as the amount that the pole is bent at the instant of take off—is governed by the forces he exerts on the pole once it is firmly "seated" against the back of the box. The forces involved may be divided into two categories—those that act across the line of the pole (the perpendicular forces) and those that act down the pole (the parallel forces). The first of these are due to the vaulter, intentionally or unintentionally, exerting an upward and forward force with his lower hand and a downward and backward force with his upper hand. This combination of forces (correctly termed a couple) exerted against a pole which is fixed at one end serves to introduce a bend into the pole. The main source of pole-bend at take off, however, is the forces generated by the vaulter's forward driving action at take off and exerted parallel to the long axis of the pole.

Although one normally thinks of a pendulum as a swinging body suspended from some fixed point, it is customary (and technically correct) to refer to the motions of the vaulter and the pole (once the vaulter has left the ground) in terms of a double pendulum—one pendulum consisting of the man rotating about a transverse axis through his hands (the man pendulum) and the other, the man and pole rotating upward about a transverse axis through the base of the pole (the man-and-pole pendulum).

Because any change in the body position of the vaulter inevitably alters the moment of inertia of each pendulum and thus the rate at which it

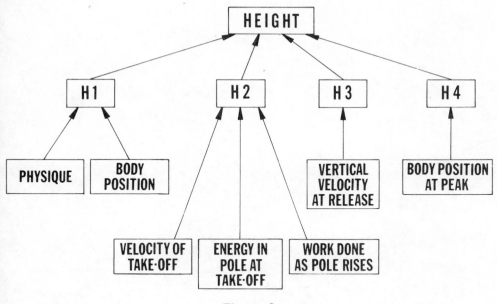

Figure 8

is swinging upward (i.e. its angular velocity) it can readily be seen that the motions of the two pendulums are interdependent. For example, if a beginning vaulter pulled-up on his arms and assumed a tucked body position immediately after take off—as beginning vaulters all too frequently do—he would simultaneously increase the moment of inertia of the man-and-pole pendulum and slow its rise toward the vertical and decrease the moment of inertia of the man pendulum and speed its forward and upward swing. Such a sequence of events completely reverses that sought by the skilled vaulter who deliberately keeps his body extended during the early stages of the vault, thus keeping the pole moving quickly towards the vertical and his body behind the pole in position for an efficient swing-up. Then, as the pole nears the vertical, the vaulter quickly swings his legs upward and momentarily assumes a tucked position prior to pulling on his arms and driving his legs upward in front of the bar. This series of actions, which slows the upward motion of the man-and-pole pendulum at the same time as it speeds the man pendulum, carries the vaulter into that position from which he finally projects himself into the air and over the bar.

The relationships between the height cleared in a pole vault and those factors discussed here which influence that height are shown diagrammatically in Figure 8.

17

THE HIGH JUMP:
STRADDLE STYLE

Athlete: **Juri Tarmak,** *U.S.S.R.*

Olympic Competition:
High Jump	1972	1st	7 feet 3¾ inches (2.23m.)

Author: **Geoffrey Dyson** is without doubt the world's leading authority on track and field techniques. Currently Director of Physical Education at Winchester College, England, President of the British Association of National Coaches and an Honorary Member of the International Olympic Academy, Dyson was formerly Chief National Coach of the A.A.A., England (1947-1961), Coach of British Olympic Games teams (1952, 1956, and 1960) and National Director of the Royal Canadian Legion's Sports Training Plan (1963-1968). His classic work, *The Mechanics of Athletics*, now in its 6th edition, has been translated into French and Japanese and is required reading in many universities.

Figure 1   **Figure 2**   **Figure 3**   **Figure 4**

Juri Tarmak, U.S.S.R., cleared 7 feet 3¾ inches (2.23m.) in Munich to become the 1972 Olympic High Jump Champion, defeating no less than eighteen other jumpers who, in the qualifying round, were required to jump 7 feet and ½ inch (2.15 m.). The Estonian—a model of Soviet jumping orthodoxy—then weighed 161 pounds (73kg.), standing 6 feet 4 inches (1.93m.).

Tarmak, the third U.S.S.R. athlete to win the Olympic high jumping crown over the last four Olympics, led up to the Munich contest with twenty-five other competitions in 1972. Strong and flexible, he uses a right-leg take off (as do a minority of jumpers) and a somewhat longer approach than most Straddle jumpers—commencing his run-up close to the outside of the track (lane 7) in Munich.

Figure 8   **Figure 9**   **Figure 10**

Figure 5   **Figure 6**   **Figure 7**

Figure 1 His run-up is approximately at a 20 degree angle to the plane of the uprights. Properly employed, this running approach will (a) increase his take-off impulse, imparting maximum vertical speed to his center of gravity (b) provide just sufficient horizontal motion for crossing the bar and (c) build up the required body-rotation for layout and bar clearance. He jogs the first few strides and then strides hard over the final eight; the early part of the run-up merely gets him into position for the all-important last three strides, without tension.

Figures 2-5 His last three strides are all over 7 feet, with the longest the penultimate; and as these are taken Tarmak lowers and advances his hips (Figures 3-5). Here, the natural left arm coordination is interrupted in preparation for an accelerated arm-circling motion which will accom-

Figure 11   **Figure 12**   **Figure 13**   **Figure 14**

pany the final spring from the ground. An early backward thrust from the arms assists in the advancement of the hips and a fast, low placement of the jumping foot, heel first.

Figures 6-7 The hips attain their lowest position through a pivoting over a maintained flexed left leg (Figure 6) and fixed ankle. (The left knee bend here is almost 90 degrees.) The circular arm movement builds up, now with the arms widespread (Figure 7).

Figures 8-11 The important take off: Now, synchronised free leg and arms accelerate upwards against the support of a flexed (approximately 130 degree at the knee) jumping leg, building up the take-off impulse. Then, with the center of gravity over this leg and fast moving upwards, an additional impulse will be applied through a vigorous extension of the torso and that leg. Note that the essential ''lay back'' position (Figure 8) has derived from an *acceleration of hips and legs—not* a deliberate straightening of the trunk.

Figure 9 Early free leg speed is essential; see how quickly it swings from the hips forward-upward; it is flexed just sufficiently to clear its foot from the ground (Figures 9 and 10). From behind, it begins bent and remains so in passing the other leg but, on reaching a horizontal position, it locks naturally and momentarily at the knee—when it should be moving at its maximum vertical speed.

Free leg and arm accelerations initiate a twisting of the trunk about its long axis (essential to an effective layout and bar clearance, later) in addition to adding to the take-off impulse.

Figure 11 Here, the Olympic Champion's position is excellent, indicating the proper execution of all previous phases of technique. His

Figure 15   **Figure 16**   **Figure 17**

center of gravity is as high as it can possibly be before actually leaving the ground; he has only a slight lean in the direction of the nearer upright, indicating rotation about a medial (i.e. fore and aft) axis—essential to his clearance half a second later. Note that the jumping leg straightens powerfully (Figures 10 and 11) only after the free leg and arm accelerations have died.

Figures 12-16 Most of Tarmak's movements in the air are a function of his run-up and take off; so what happens now is largely predetermined, as, certainly, is the flight path of his center of gravity. But to a limited extent he *can* initiate movement in the air (which will, of course, have its equal and opposite reaction within his body) which can change his position relative to his center of gravity and affect his rotation about an axis (of momentum) fixed in direction and passing through that center of gravity.

Figure 12 Momentarily, the jumping leg is permitted to "hang," so as to advance his upper body and hips relative to his center of gravity. At this stage the free leg flexes again, with its thigh fairly close to Tarmak's chest—but with its foot higher than the knee and directed towards (and slightly above) the crossbar. The left arm also reaches towards the bar.

Figure 13 We can see the beginnings of a layout, as the jumping leg flexes and the more compact body position speeds up rotation about the medial axis. Left arm, free leg and upper trunk continue to lead across the bar; chest and leading thigh maintain their "piked" relationship.

Figure 14 Tarmak's rotation to the right is further increased as the jumping leg folds markedly. The head and shoulders are raised no more than necessary. Note the commencement of a straightening of the free leg

Figure 18   **Figure 19**   **Figure 20**

at hip and knee and its movement to the left—which, in reaction, swings the trunk into a more parallel position to the crossbar.

Figure 15 The horizontal position shown speeds up Tarmak's twist about the bar (Figures 15-18), making easier the clearing of a well-flexed jumping leg. However, he also makes an effort to lift its knee (Figures 16 and 17) "against" a contrary twisting of the upper body; so, momentarily, his trunk twist away from the bar is delayed. The 1972 Olympic Champion is content with a layout in which there is little body-mass below bar level at the high point of the jump (Figures 15 and 16); he makes no noticeable attempt to drape his body abound the bar.

Figures 18–20 The rotation developed at take off continues, so that he lands on his back.

18

THE HIGH JUMP: FLOP STYLE

Athlete: **Ulrike Meyfahrt,** *West Germany*

Olympic Competition:
High Jump	1972	1st	6 feet 3½ inches (1.92 m.)
			(World Record)

Author: **Berny Wagner**, track coach at Oregon State University, is one of the nation's outstanding college coaches—his athletes have won more individual N.C.A.A. championships over the past 5 years than have those of any other school. Among the many outstanding athletes he has produced are Dick Fosbury, 1968 Olympic high jump champion and originator of the Fosbury Flop style of jumping; and Tom Woods and John Radetich, outstanding exponents of that style.

Figure 1 This shows Ulrike Meyfahrt in full sprinting stride on her toes. She is turning to her left (note right knee coming across toward the midline) and starting to draw back her left arm to put it in synchronization with her right arm for double-arm take-off action. She is looking at the bar.

Figure 2 Meyfahrt is starting her "settle" changing from sprint action to a flat-footed running action and lowering her hips, but keeping the upper body upright. Note the dorsal flexion of her right foot to accomplish this. Her hands are wide and in back for double arm take-off action.

Figure 3 She is in a flat-foot, knee-bent, and hips-lowered "settle"

Figure 1   **Figure 2**   **Figure 3**

Figure 7   **Figure 8**   **Figure 9**   **Figure 10**

position. Her right arm starts forward, but the left arm and hand is delayed and stays back.

Figure 4 Meyfahrt pushes off her right toe vigorously into the last step. Her hips are still slightly lowered and body upright. Her right hand and arm are carried forward in normal action, but the left arm and hand are still delayed. It is here that one can see that although she prepared for a double-arm take-off action, she is not using one. The left arm and hand come forward much slower than the right. The angle of the right foot indicates that she is still turning on her approach.

Figure 5 Meyfahrt is almost at her "plant" position. This picture seems to indicate that she lands with a heel-first plant. Her body is leaning

Figure 4   **Figure 5**   **Figure 6**

Figure 11   **Figure 12**   **Figure 13**   **Figure 14**

back as hips stay low and forward of the shoulders. Her right arm and hand are still swinging up, but the left is still slowed and delayed. She appears to be planting her take-off foot parallel to the crossbar.

Figure 6 This photo shows the take-off position. The take-off leg is bent as a result of the lowered hip position or "settle." The right arm extends up and toward the bar to help initiate rotation around the horizontal axis. The right knee is driven up with the foot staying back under the hips as with the start of lead-leg action in hurdle clearance. Her take-off foot is parallel to the bar and she takes off close to the standard, rather than near the middle of the bar. It seems that she starts leaning toward the bar a trifle too soon on this jump. Her left arm flexes at the elbow and is brought across the body but not up in a double arm take-off action.

Figure 7 Meyfahrt has begun extension of the take-off leg and plantar flexion has begun with the take-off foot. The right, or lead, foot stays behind the right knee as knee drive is decreased or stopped. The knee starts across the body slightly, but the foot continues in the line of its original motion which was that of the approach on the final step, and apparently parallel to the crossbar. The right arm continues reaching (extending) up and toward the bar. Her body leans slightly toward the bar (following the lead arm) to initiate rotation around the horizontal axis at the hips, which gives rotation over the bar. She has been looking at the bar on her last two steps and continues to do so throughout the take off. The left arm, elbow bent, still comes up, but only chest high in spite of the fact that the knee drive is at an end. She must get a strong rotation around the vertical axis at this phase of her jump. It is obvious from this

| Figure 15 | Figure 16 | Figure 17 | Figure 18 |

and subsequent pictures that it is not initiated by an arm or leg drive across the body from right to left, because she actually "turns away" from her lead knee and arm, and then brings them back to the midline (Figures 7-10).

Figures 8-9 The right arm leads over the bar, and the left arm finally reaches its highest point—about shoulder high and well across the body. Note the position of her knees as she has "turned away" from her right or lead leg as the knee and foot have continued on the path of the approach. There is good, full extension of the take-off leg and full plantar flexion in the take-off foot. The upper body is just starting vertical axis rotation, although the take-off leg is fully rotated away from the bar. She is starting to rotate around the horizontal axis through her hips, while extending and dropping her right knee.

Figures 10-11 Meyfahrt's upper body catches up with her lower body in the vertical axis rotation. Her left knee is just now pointing in the same direction as her right knee. Her right foot is still being pulled back toward the midline and rotation away from the bar. This last is not accomplished yet. Her right arm is abducted out at right angles to her body. This arm action slows rotation around the vertical axis. Her chin is on her collar bone and she is still looking at the bar. In Figure 11 she has rotated past the position of facing directly away from the bar. Her right knee is as extended as it will get.

Figures 12-13 These pictures show continued backward rotation around the horizontal axis. The effect of too much vertical axis rotation is shown by the fact that her left hip is now lower than her right. She is still

| **Figure 19** | **Figure 20** | **Figure 21** | **Figure 22** |

fighting this with her arms. Her hips are pushed forward for bar clearance. She is still looking at the bar over her right shoulder, chin on collar bone until her hips are at the bar.

Figures 14-15 Meyfahrt shows good back arch starting here. Horizontal axis rotation has continued. The hips are still rising. She has finally brought the vertical axis rotation under control by moving her left arm back to the left across her body. The right foot is finally brought into a bilaterally symmetrical position with the left. Maximum height is reached in Figure 15 as hips are over the bar. She is clearing the bar near the center (the lowest part of the bar) because of her take off near the standard rather than in the center of the take-off area is shown.

Figure 16 The left hip has been raised even with the right by moving the left arm downward and to the left. Hip flexion is initiated here as the knees are flexed.

Figures 17-18 Meyfahrt's hips are dropped, and as a reaction lower legs can be raised. The knees begin to extend. Her chin is brought forward toward the chest as the neck is flexed.

Figure 19 This photo shows Meyfahrt's knees being extended vigorously as descent into the pit continues.

Figures 20-22 These photos show the drop to the landing area and the landing on her back. Note she keeps her chin down.

19

THE POLE VAULT

Athlete: **Wolfgang Nordwig,** *East Germany*

Olympic Competition:

Pole Vault	1968	3rd	17 feet 8½ inches (5.40 m.)
Pole Vault	1972	1st	18 feet ½ inch (5.50 m.)
			(Olympic Record)

Author: **Geoff Elliott**, is an Associate Professor of Physical Education at the University of Alberta. A former British Commonwealth Games champion (1954, 1958) and European Championships medallist (1954) in the pole vault, Elliott is widely recognized as a leading authority on the jumping events.

Figures 1-4 In these pictures of the penultimate stride the pole has already reached a horizontal position and is being lowered from there. The right hand moves from just behind the hip to above the head, in a straight line. This ensures that the front end of the pole is not moved forward (in relation to the body) and then brought back again hence hitting the back of the box prematurely. The hands do not move their position on the pole at all during this phase. The elbows should be facing forward rather than outward over the next stride. In order to produce the planting move efficiently the shoulders themselves must be pulled out of line with the hips and an unfortunate consequence of this is that the right foot may be swung across the body. The misplacing of the right foot from the line of run can cause the vaulter to be off balance. The

Figure 1   **Figure 2**   **Figure 3**

shoulders come very quickly back in line as soon as the right hand has passed the shoulder so that on the last stride the shoulders, legs, hips and feet are in excellent balanced driving positions.

Figure 5 If a vertical line were drawn from the top hand it would not pass through the left foot position that is shown, whereas if a vertical line were drawn from the left hand it would go through this position. In some instances criticism could be made of this position if one were not aware of the actual take-off position shown in the next photograph. The good points of this position are indicated in the flexed right leg thus allowing a very fast movement of the right leg and also the flexed right and left arms, thus being in a position to absorb much of the shock of the pole hitting the end of the box.

Figure 6 This is an excellent position which many coaches should try to get their athletes to emulate. The take off is directly below the upper hand. The upper arm is flexed, this is most important at this stage because the weight of the body now can be absorbed by tension in the arm muscles rather than the whole body, which would tend to be snatched off the ground prematurely. The left arm is in a good position in that it is acting as a strut (note it is not straight) thus preventing the shoulders from swinging ahead of the hands too early in this and subsequent stages. The right thigh has been picked up to a position which is indicative of one of horizontal drive as opposed to lift. In the classic lifting phase one would expect to see the right thigh horizontal or above with the lower leg swung much further forward perhaps at a right angle with the knee. However,

Figure 4 **Figure 5** **Figure 6**

because the vaulter is interested in maintaining a lot of horizontal drive the thigh is not driven that high.

There is a tendency to neglect the importance of this and the earlier stages of vaulting shown in Figures 1-6, yet it is quite evident that the vault is generally made or lost in this area—take off being most critical. There are some small things that a vaulter may do to save a vault if there have been some incorrect movements prior to this but in general the chances are minimal. A vaulter and his coach have to do much analysis of the positions that he demonstrates through Figures 5 and 6.

Figure 7 Now the athlete is off the ground and, inevitably, the right arm taking the full weight of the body is stretched to its athletic limit. This, of course, will produce a force on the pole which helps to encourage a greater bend. This is in addition to the forward motion of the athlete which will produce a bend in the pole, providing the athlete can allow this to occur by ensuring that the left arm is still acting as a strut and making sure that the body, hips and legs do not move through too quickly at this stage in the vault. Failure to keep the body back in this way detracts from the bend in the pole.

Figure 8 The athlete has one of two options left to him depending on the flexibility of his pole. One is that he can increase the bend of the pole by lifting the legs vigorously and as straight as possible. This will ensure a greater bend in the pole and hence allow it to store greater energy. However, if the pole is not able to do this the athlete, by lifting in this position, will merely delay the pole straightening out. This latter may be

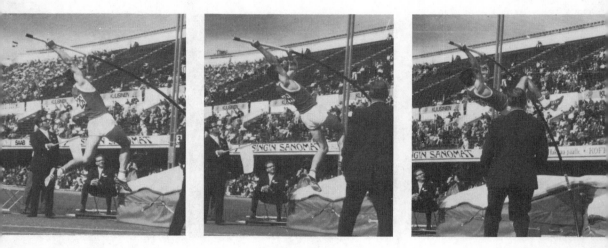

Figure 7   **Figure 8**   **Figure 9**

the more desirable alternative because the inference is that the athlete is capable of using a stiffer pole. If the stiffer pole will give back to the vaulter greater kinetic energy from its stored potential energy then this is highly desirable, particularly if it gives it back very rapidly. Most vaulters are familiar with the pole that bends too much, stays bent, and gives back its energy very slowly and, of course, in an event where a vaulter is working against the forces of gravity this can be a serious disadvantage. The moral is the stiffer the pole, all other things being equal, the better the vaulter, and the better the vault. Note in particular the vaulter has allowed the take-off leg to almost catch up with the lead leg at this stage. The trunk has stayed in its same relative position to the pole and is to all practical purposes still in its take-off position.

Figures 9-10 The vigorous lifting of the legs produces a reaction through the hands which encourages the maintenance of bend in the pole. (If the pole is too flexible it will increase the bend in the pole.) If this movement is done correctly it will keep the trunk back in line. It is interesting to note the head position here. Some coaches have stated that the head should be dropped back in order that the trunk can be brought back and a rocking movement produced. In effect, however, if the head is pushed back there is an actual reflex action which tends to make the body arch and thus the angle is taken out of the shoulders which would be most undesirable. If the head is kept in a curled position the trunk too tends to

Figure 10   Figure 11   Figure 12   Figure 13

be curled, which is far more natural position for the vaulter to be in; also, it is a happier position for the vaulter as he tends to be in a kinesthetically better position. It should be pointed out at this stage that the vaulter, if he has little "space awareness," has only contact with the ground through his hands, and as the pole is bent and away from the body, the images that the vaulter is perceiving through his hands are the ones that the coach has to try to understand. It may be that the vaulter does not relate to the ground or to the stands or to the crossbar but rather to the position of his hands. If the head is lined up with the background it is interesting to note that the vaulter's head in fact moves down in Figure 10 from Figure 8 and then goes up a little in Figure 11 and, of course, starts to rise quickly in Figure 12 as the pole straightens out. The position of the vaulter is almost underneath the bar and the impression that the vaulter gets from take off which is some 12 feet away from the box is that he is traveling horizontally, for an awfully long period of time.

Figure 11 This shows another critical phase of the vault. The vaulter now must make some sort of attempt at keeping the legs in a vertical position and at the same time extend the trunk from its back-lying position into a complete upside-down position. The difference between a beginning vaulter and an experienced vaulter here is that the experienced vaulter will maintain his feet in a vertical position over his hips as he is holding on to the pole. The pole at this stage should be giving back in a

Figure 14   **Figure 15**   **Figure 16**   **Figure 17**

vertical direction all of the energy which he has transmitted to it in the earlier phases of the vault. The position shows the knees and the hands very close together and although the body is moving upwards fairly fast there is no indication of a pulling action by the athlete. In fact, if a pull (in the sense of flexing the arms) is executed at this stage the pole would tend not to straighten out but to stay bent which, of course, could be disastrous for the athlete.

Figure 12 The pole is almost straight at this point and the athlete must now start to think about the rotation of the body about its longitudinal axis in order that he may turn over to clear the bar face downwards.

The vaulter has crossed the right leg over the left hence initiating some rotation and is in a good straight position (with a low moment of inertia) to make the turning easier.

Figure 13 The legs have strayed apart just a little here and this is to the athlete's disadvantage except that it does help in slowing down the rotation and perhaps giving the athlete slightly better stability.

Figure 14 The great tendency for average vaulters at this time in the vault is for the legs to drop away from the pole and hence detract from any possibility of utilizing the arms in a pulling and pushing movement. It is towards the end of the rotation, when the athlete should be moving in a vertical direction under the velocity that has been imparted to his body by the straightening of the pole, that the first suggestion of pulling should

Figure 18   **Figure 19**   **Figure 20**

occur. In most cases the success or failure of a vault depends on the position of the foot closest to the bar in this picture. The vaulter very often, if he is guilty of an early pike, will hit the bar. Yet the body position over the bar would indicate that it is quite easy for the vaulter to clear the bar by a foot or so. The vaulter must be very cognizant of his position in relation to the bar. It takes a lot of extremely good first-class vaulting to get this sort of feeling.

Figures 15-16 The largest problem the vaulter faces at this stage of the vault is the body going away from the pole with the feet dropping too soon, thus creating a tremendous tendency for backward rotation in the athlete and hence the dropping of the hips on to the bar. Many texts tell of the strong action required in pushing and pulling through these phases yet if the preliminary actions are performed correctly this aspect of the vault should not be accentuated. The important aspect of this phase of the vault is to keep the body as compact as possible until such time as the hips are in a position over the bar.

Figure 17 The athlete can concentrate on clearing the chest and arms since his body is in a good compact position. The techniques that have been talked about in the past for rigid-pole vaulting apply as well for flexible-pole vaulting in bar clearance in that the chest should be caved with the body forming an arch and the elbows turned outwards to ensure that the athlete does not contact the bar with either the elbows or hands.

Figures 18-20 Once the athlete's center of gravity is clear of and past the bar the athlete is capable of performing a backward movement of the feet in relation to the trunk so assisting the head, chest and arms to go in a backward movement thus ensuring that they do clear the bar. The danger of performing this movement too early is of course that the hips are depressed or pushed forward on to the bar. The problem of pushing the hips forward will ensure that the bar stays on the uprights whereas depressing the bar merely makes it bounce and stay or bounce and topple.

20

THE LONG JUMP: HITCH-KICK STYLE

Athlete: **Randy Williams,** *U.S.A.*

Olympic Competition:
  Long Jump   1972   1st   27 feet ½ inch (8.24 m.)

Author: **Ken Bosen** is coach of the Tata Iron and Steel Co., Ltd., Jamshedpur, India. He has had a distinguished career in track and field over the past 25 years. He established an Indian national record in the javelin (1950); instructed at the National Coaching Camps of the Amateur Athletic Federation of India (1962 to the present); was appointed first National Coach of the A.A.F.I. (1969-70); instructed at a national clinic in the U.S.A. (1964); served as Coach of the Indian team at the Olympic Games (1964); and gained first-place honors in the track and field diploma course at East Germany's D.H.f.K. (1965). Bosen has also contributed extensively to the literature on track and field.

Though the photo sequence does not include frames of the approach run, it will not be out of place to mention that the accumulation of maximum horizontal velocity in the run-up must culminate in an uninhibited take-off action—to ensure full continuity in the changing of the forces of the run-up to the forces at the take off. Though there is a loss of forward velocity in the next-to-last stride before the take off, this cannot be seen in a photo study. However, to cut deceleration to a minimum, the good jumper compromises so that his velocity at take off is approximately two to one in favor of the horizontal rather than the vertical. This means that great explosive power must be developed during the take off to avoid sacrificing forward momentum while obtaining lift in the split second that is at the disposal of the jumper at the take-off board.

The last two or three strides before the take off are by no means consistently the same for the same jumper let alone for different jumpers. The pattern of these last few strides should be interpreted with care in training, as the preparations for the lift, though hardly noticeable in good jumpers, are nevertheless there if suitable photos are available to cover these final steps of the approach and the actions at take off. The "settle" or "gather" as this phase is termed, should never be interpreted as a slowing-down of the run-up to get lift. A jumper neither concentrates on shortening nor on lengthening these last strides to form a particular pattern. Actually, top-class jumpers ignore the idea of any fixed stride pattern in these last strides. Their physical preparations include a naturally more upright position of the trunk as they sink slightly over the nontake-

Figure 1   Figure 2   Figure 3   Figure 4

off leg, thereby permitting the take-off foot to reach slightly ahead of the jumper's center of gravity for better forward-upward drive from the take-off board. This brings the jumper into a position to use his take-off forces to an optimum regardless of whether the last strides before the take off are shortened or lengthened.

The jumper is concerned with two major tasks during the take off. He must obtain good vertical lift from the take-off board and he must maintain as much of his horizontal speed as possible. All this must be executed within the fraction of a second that the jumper's take-off foot is in contact with the board. The change from horizontal speed to vertical is achieved, therefore, by application of the maximum forces from the take-off leg.

Figures 1-4 The jumper is about to complete his last stride, with body erect, chin slightly up and eyes looking upward-forward. This indicates a sense of confidence in the jumper's ability to hit the take-off board in a consistent run-up to the board. Figure 1 shows Randy Williams coming onto the take-off board with the foot well ahead of the body's center of gravity as it strikes the take-off mark. The take-off foot in Figure 2 shows good flat-footed placement, covering the board's width nicely, while the swinging leg has been left well behind, with the heel high to the rear as it is swung through to assist in creating vertical lift and minimizing forward rotation through a bent high-knee lift action as seen in Figure 3. As the center of gravity passes the vertical plane of the foot in contact with the take-off board (Figures 2-3), the take-off leg flexes slightly at the knee joint to reduce resistance to forward motion and start the vertical

Figure 5   Figure 6   Figure 7   Figure 8

drive seen in Figures 3-4. Notice the left knee flexion through Figures 2-4 and note the center of gravity move forward as the take-off knee straightens and lifts the bulk of the hips forward-upwards into the flight. This drive is strongly assisted by the free leg swing which swings from well behind in Figure 1 to well forward-upwards in Figure 4. The short pendulum action of the free leg swing as seen in Figures 1-4 permits the free leg to move at remarkable speed. This action of the free leg swing is well-coordinated with the actions of the two arms in an alternate type arm swing used by most American jumpers. The good hip and chest lift seen from Figures 2-6 shows the power behind Williams' take-off actions. The vigorous extension of the take-off leg, having used every available force to propel him forward-upwards, has been completed in Figure 4 where it can be seen that the jumper has finally lost contact with the take-off board, and the flight path of the center of gravity has been determined.

The main objective of using a particular style in flight is to absorb the rotation developed at take off. The movement of the jumper's limbs during the flight helps in flight balance and stability. It is argued that the absorption of forward rotation through the vigorous actions of the free leg swing and proper use of the two arms at the take off is manifest in an efficient lift of the two legs at the landing. There are those who argue that the actions of these limbs at the take off create even a certain amount of backward rotation while they absorb whatever forward rotation is created, and it is this factor that makes for good leg lift at the landing.

Randy Williams uses a hitch-kick method which is seen in his flight

Figure 9   **Figure 10**   **Figure 11**   **Figure 12**

from Figures 5-15. Though his form in flight is really of secondary importance, it is worthy of note that it conforms to the accepted principles which permit a smooth take off, good balance in flight, and make it possible for him to secure an excellent landing position.

Figures 5-15 Williams has left the take-off board with a slight forward rotation in Figure 5 and starts to absorb it by creating local rotations around his center of gravity through the hitch-kick movements. Figures 5-8 show that the hitch-kick begins with the free leg moving down and backwards in a long lever action while the take-off leg, flexed in reaction to the drive, is brought forward as a short lever. The arms, supporting the actions vigorously, help with balance and also contribute slightly towards efforts to create a backward rotation. Figures 6 and 11 show the typical long pendular movements that only the hitch-kick jumper attains in midflight. Meanwhile, Figures 9-14 show the second aspect of the flight in which the body has begun to take on a slight backward lean. The arms, which alternated earlier, move into a double arm swing from Figure 10-17, while the take-off (left) leg begins to move downward and backward in a long lever and the right leg starts to flex in a short lever and move forward (Figures 10-14). It is the actions of the two arms in Figures 10-13 that give the jumper's upper body the slight backward lean seen in Figures 11-13. Figures 13-15 show the completion of the hitch-kick actions as the bent legs move forward-upwards for the landing in coordination with the forward-downwards sweep of the two arms and upper body.

The main aim of the jumper in the landing is to achieve a position

Figure 13   Figure 14   Figure 15   Figure 16

with the feet far forward of his center of gravity without falling back in the pit. While it is true that the arc traveled by the jumper's center of gravity is predetermined, the actual distance jumped can be lessened or increased by the position of the body and legs at the moment of the landing in the pit.

Figures 16-20 In continuation with the actions of the two legs and arms described in the flight phase earlier, Figures 16-17 show Williams' two arms swinging well behind the hips. This action takes his upper body forward more than is desirable at this point. However, his two legs are well up in Figure 17 and the two feet are not too widely spread either. It might have been better had his hitch-kick actions not ended as early as seen in this photo sequence. It is usually the case that the legs tend to drop early if the hitch-kick actions end sooner than necessary. This then is the advantage of doing the Boston, Davies or Ter-Ovanesian types of hitch-kick actions. Figures 18-20 show Williams using a wide lateral sweep of his two arms and a forward body tuck position to help his recovery so as to avoid sitting back in the pit. These photos show good flexion at the knees while the buttocks just graze the top of the sand pit to make the forward plunge seen in Figure 20. It appears that the jumper's heels have broken the sand well in advance of the trunk. This might have been more obvious had there been one more frame between Figures 17 and 18. However, the landing has been successfully completed here as the body is seen to pivot over the flexed knees with a certain effort as seen in Figure 19, which may be indicative of the fact that his legs did not drop too much before he hit the sand pit.

Figure 17   **Figure 18**   **Figure 19**   **Figure 20**

21

THE LONG JUMP: HANG STYLE

Athlete: **Heide Rosendahl,** *West Germany*

Olympic Competition:

Long Jump	1972	1st	22 feet 3 inches (6.78 m.)
4 x 100m.	1972	1st	42.8 (Equal World Record)
Pentathlon	1972	2nd	4791 points

Author: **Gerd Osenberg**, West Germany, has been coach of his country's national team in various international matches, at the European Championships (1967, 1971) and at the Olympic Games (1968, 1972). Heide Rosendahl is one of many world class athletes he has coached.

By means of her training as an all-round athlete, Heide Rosendahl was able to compensate for a weakness frequently occurring to women jumpers—the lack of strength in the mid-torso. A further prerequisite for her Olympic victory was her sprinting power at the right time (200m. in the pentathlon in 22.96 seconds and a good finish as the final runner in the victorious 4 x 100m. relay prove this).

Unfortunately the most important factor, the run-up, cannot be evaluated from this series of pictures. From memory I must say that Heide is competent in her run-up (9 valid attempts out of 10—1 qualifying, 3 in preliminaries, 3 in finals, 3 in pentathlon) but she is not perfect. She did

Figure 1

Figure 2

Figure 3

Figure 4

Figure 9

Figure 10

Figure 11

Figure 12

not find the optimum jump-preparation from her high running speed. Thus one can see from the series of pictures that the take off from the board was a little hasty. This error becomes visible in the difficulty to extend the flight-phase (Figures 6-8) and to delay the landing (Figures 13-15). One can see very clearly in Figures 1-4 that Heide does not sink in the knees and thus preserves her energy of motion completely. Likewise good—on the basis of her previously-mentioned torso-strength—is no backward-bending of the upper body into a hollow-back position, so that the legs can be brought in good relation to the perpendicular torso (Figures 10-11).

To make reference to Heide's training would mean to see her as a

Figure 5   **Figure 6**   **Figure 7**   **Figure 8**

Figure 13   **Figure 14**   **Figure 15**   **Figure 16**

pentathlon competitor and not as a long-jumper, for surely more than 60 percent of her training was dedicated to the weak exercises in shot-put and high-jump. To this was added a use of 15 percent for hurdles. Thus 25 percent of her training is used for sprinting, strength, and jump-training. This makes 2½ hours in a total of about 10 hours training per week in winter, and in summer 4 hours per week in a total 16-hour training.

In strength-training Heide prefers rapid-strength exercises, for example the jerk up to 25kg. In jumping-training, she prefers multiple jumps right, left, left, right, landing. In running-training, she practices tempo-runs between 100-300m. in which the tempo in winter of a 200m. run is about 28 seconds, in summer about 25 seconds. Number of repeats is 3-5.

Figure 17   **Figure 18**   **Figure 19**   **Figure 20**

22

THE TRIPLE JUMP

Athlete: **Viktor Saneyev,** *U.S.S.R.*

Olympic Competition:

Triple Jump	1968	1st	57 feet ¾ inches (17.39m.)
			(World Record)
Triple Jump	1972	1st	56 feet 11 inches (17.35m.)

Author: **John Powell** is Chairman of the Department of Human Kinetics and Director of the School of Physical Education at the University of Guelph, Canada. A former decathlon champion and English representative in gymnastics, he was head coach of track and field at Cambridge University, England (1947) and at Rhodes University, South Africa (1948-60). He is the author of *Track and Field Fundamentals for Teacher and Coach* and of approximately 100 articles on track and field; and has instructed at numerous coaching clinics in England, South Africa, the United States and Canada.

Before attempting to concentrate on
an analysis, the reader is encouraged to glance from the first to the
twenty-ninth photograph as though scanning the pages of a book to per-
ceive the total impression of this triple action blended into one whole
movement.

At the outset, it is as well to appreciate that this is but one effort at
the triple jump in the lifetime of an exceptional athlete. Furthermore,
while it is true that the whole action is made up of parts it is vital to
understand that in the context of an athletic effort the whole is *more* than
just the sum of the parts. As we go through this splendid performance and
identify factors it should be recognized that, in the *complete* performance
(viewed at the speed of that performance), the various separate aspects are
not at all evident—quite a different impression of a continuous, rhythmic,
powerful action is received than when the self-same effort is analyzed
frame by frame.

Careful analysis through the camera's eye will demonstrate how, in
regard to timing and degree, quantity and quality, certain aspects contribute to the complete, blended effort.

It is assumed this left to right series was photographed from a fixed
point at a constant rate of frames per second.

THE RUN-UP

The run-up (not shown) is an integral part of the performance. This
run-up was from 15 running paces, sprinting speed (not "full out" but
fast and controlled) was attained prior to the athlete's striking the board.

Before following the analysis, take a red pencil and carefully mark
with a ruler the top of the head of the athlete throughout the whole series
in your book. Thorough understanding of this performance involves ap-
preciation of the particular technique Saneyev is using. The red line
drawn throughout the series will indicate graphically the shallow type of
progression he adopts, in which he advances so smoothly and yet dramatically from one phase of this triple movement to another.

THE HOP

Look at Figure 2, in which the athlete has just struck the board;
observe the foot position which is flat, the knee over the toes, the upright
trunk position, the eyes directed well ahead. Figure 2 shows the gathering
of the body's forces for the effort to come. Note the erectness of the body,
the right flat foot, the gaze, and the balanced position. Look at Figure 3;
the red line indicates a remarkable angle of increase as the body mass has
passed over the supporting foot which is driving *forward-upward*.

The most exciting photograph so far is Figure 4: freezing motion

Figure 1 **Figure 2** **Figure 3**

with a superb extension of the driving right leg, high, powerful knee lift with lower left leg relaxed, the stretch of the body, strong counter-arm action, ever erect body and forward gaze.

Figure 5 identifies the automatic relaxation of the right leg as a result of its follow through, occasioned by the mighty drive it has exerted. The red line shows the gradual mounting of the head; the forward-upward surge can also be observed by noting progressive position of the athlete's left thigh relative to seated officials in Figures 5, 6, and 7.

Now look at Figure 6 where, because the left leg has started to

Figure 4 **Figure 5** **Figure 6**

Figure 7   **Figure 8**   **Figure 9**

extend down, so the right arm (to counter-balance this longer lower limb movement and preserve balance) has also extended. From this point on note how the arms are used in a more extended way. This is a learned technique, not a natural one—although certainly efficient. The use of long arm levers has an arresting action on the lower limbs, thus, no movement in this whole sequence is hurried. The timing of the drive of one phase into another keeps continuity and the long arm levers ensure that enough time is given for full execution of every detail.

The seventh picture is revealing. It indicates the height of the hop

Figure 13   **Figure 14**   **Figure 15**

Figure 10   **Figure 11**   **Figure 12**

phase, the excellent balancing of arms and legs and a controlled position without tension. The trunk is correctly erect. Figure 8 allows observation of the preparatory gearing of the whole body for the landing from the first part of this triple effort, the right arm is being extended back, quite loosely, as will be identified by lack of muscle definition.

In Figure 9 there is a more rigid stretching back of the right arm to compensate for the right leg's going forward, but there is no overstretching.

Figure 10 should be carefully noted because the head position indi-

Figure 16   **Figure 17**   **Figure 18**

Figure 19   **Figure 20**   **Figure 21**

cates a "settling" of the body. Counter-balancing of the long right lower limb through the action of the long right arm is noticeable.

Figure 12. The right foot is flat on the run-up in order to give the greatest surface area possible for the forward-backward balance necessary in this transition phase. Splendid control exists when the body is erect; all the lever actions have been reduced and resistance is slight to the transitional movement. Look back and feel the flow of movement through Figures 10, 11 and 12.

THE STEP

Figure 12 shows how the center of mass of the body has been quickly transferred over, forward from the foot, forcing the athlete on, as seen in Figure 13 where again you will observe a raising of the red line.

Generally, it is not wise to compare one photograph with another because the purposes of the movement shown may be different, yet it is profitable to look at the excellent extension of the whole of the right lower limb in Figure 13 and to look again at this extension in Figure 4. Because the photographer is more nearly opposite the athlete in Figure 13 it may give the impression that there is a slight forward lean of the trunk (when compared to Figure 4) but there are similarities to note.

Observe carefully Figure 14, compare it to Figure 5 where the right leg, having done its work is more relaxed and the left thigh is exactly to waist level. These actions prove there is no backward rotation. See how the arms are acting as both propellors and balancers.

The renowned Swastika position is seen clearly in Figure 15, the

Figure 22 **Figure 23** **Figure 24**

long sweeping action in the arms seem, momentarily, to give suspension of the body. All movements are blending preparatory to a controlled, compact, efficient landing.

Look at Figure 16 in which the lower limbs appear to remain in suspension yet the arms are being brought back in order that they can make contributions through their leverage, length, and mass.

Look again at the red line, note the gradual dropping of this up to Figure 20. Figure 17 is a splendid example of stretch, in all senses, not overstretch. This superb athlete exhibits control motion, preserving as much momentum as has been possible, so far. Despite the arms being back there is no forward inclination of the trunk and, in Figure 19, the left foot will be seen to have come flat to the ground, the body ready to flow its movement through into the next phase. Figure 20 can be compared to Figure 11 (although a fraction later in its photography). Look carefully at Figure 20 and note a "sinking" of the body, but the left leg is not bending unduly although the hips correctly "sag." Then, look at Figure 21.

THE LEAP

The violence of the full extension of the body is obvious. Not only is this noticeable by the sharp increase (Figures 21-22) in the angle of the red line but also by the way the arms have swept through, by the extension of the left leg and the counter-action of the right thigh. Compare Figure 21 to Figure 13. There is a remarkable similarity. *Some* momentum will, of necessity, have been lost in the process of this effort and yet the movement is under such excellent control that the athlete has been

Figure 25   **Figure 26**   **Figure 27**

able to preserve constancy of body-form and maximal drive from one phase to the next. Because of this last violent movement Figure 22 shows the most steep rise in angle of the red line. The elevation of the body by the arms is to delay (as long as possible) any forward inclination of the body, which would not only have a depression effect upon both thighs as they come through, but also would have a tendency to create a forward rotation, driving the hips back. This, in consequence, would make for a less economic landing. Look at the board behind the athlete's hips and note, in Figures 23, 24, and 25 how they have been maintained at a great height as a result of initial settling and continuous movement from Figure 20 into Figure 21.

THE LANDING

The rules stipulate that the landing be made on both feet, thus there is a technique necessary to prepare for this. It is not solely the reduction in momentum that causes the body to dip so considerably (Figures 24-29) but the employment of this technique ensures that the athlete be in the best position to extend the heels as far forward as possible and yet have enough residual energy to bend at the knees on impact and allow the body mass to work over the fulcrum of the heels.

It is essential to keep the body as erect as possible for as long as possible, and to extend the arm through as great a range as possible in order that their leverage and relative slowness of this powerful movement will give the time necessary to acquire added centimeters.

Figure 28   **Figure 29**

Look at the very last frame where the heels have landed. The arms have not yet come through but neither have the buttocks touched the sand. Again, the body is noted to be relatively erect. Study of Figure 24 shows that the movement has been superbly executed, the greatest amount of extension has been given to the limbs, resulting in the greatest amount of distance (relative to the force expended) possible.

Summary

The whole series indicates a well-controlled movement of the shallow type. Each time contact has been made with the ground new forces were originated enabling Saneyev, through his splendidly balanced action, to preserve as much continuity as possible and yet direct again and again maximum force *from a controlled position* into the next phase.

This series of photographs is an excellent example of a well-coordinated, splendidly-executed series in which the proportions of hop-step-jump are near to being perfect *for this athlete*.

Although it is not advisable for any athlete to attempt to copy another's action exactly because of so many variable factors such as opportunities for training, expert coaching, differences of physique and attitude, as well as basic speed, it is helpful to observe some common features for emulation:

1. Fast controlled approach
2. Terrific drive from the ground, forward-upward
3. Landing on a flat foot with the body very slightly behind the landing foot

4. Quick transfer into each next phase
5. Always an upright body
6. Good counter-balancing of long levers of the leg by long levers of the arm; making the most of the landing position by full extension of the lower limbs as well as full extension of the arms.

PART THREE
The Throwing Events

23

FUNDAMENTAL MECHANICS OF THROWING

Author: **Tom Ecker** has coached track and field at the junior high, high school, university, and international levels. The author of seven sports books and more than 70 technical coaching articles in national magazines, Ecker has traveled widely throughout North America and Europe, lecturing on various aspects of sport. In 1964 the U. S. State Department sent him on a ten-week coaching lecture tour of the northern European countries. In 1966-68 he served as national coach of the Swedish team.

The throwing events can be divided into two general categories—the nonaerodynamic events (the shot put and hammer throw) and the aerodynamic events (the discus throw and javelin throw).

In the nonaerodynamic events, there are only three factors that determine how far the implement will go—the speed of the implement at the moment of release, the angle of release, and the height of release. In the aerodynamic events, however, besides the speed, angle and height of release, there is one other important factor—the effect air resistance has on the implement as it travels through the air.

In each of the four throwing events, the athlete begins by imparting horizontal force to the throwing implement—toward the direction of throw in the shot and javelin, around the body's vertical axis (which allows for some simultaneous vertical force during the turning) in the discus and hammer (Figure 1). Then, just before releasing, a nearly vertical force is added. It is a great lifting force in the shot and hammer, but less in the discus and javelin, where release angles are not so high (Figure 2). The summed effect of all the horizontal and vertical forces exerted on each implement determines its angle of release and its exact speed of release.

The force exerted is dependent to a large extent upon the thrower's mass and the length of his levers. Since the reaction at the moment of release will cause less relative backward movement in his upper body, a heavier athlete can exert more effective force over a greater distance than can a lighter athlete. It is obvious, then, that in the throwing events the heavier the thrower, the more advantage he has, if all other factors are equal.

It is essential that the various body forces contributing to the throw be exerted in the proper order—timed to build on previous forces—in order to provide the greatest possible speed at release. As the implement increases in speed before its release, the parts of the body in a position to contribute must be able to move faster than the implement is already moving, if there is to be continued acceleration. This requires the larger, slower muscle groups of the athlete's body to be brought into play first, followed by the smaller, faster groups as the implement approaches maximum speed prior to release.

SPEED OF RELEASE

In all throwing events, speed of release is the most important factor. In fact, a small percentage increase in release speed will always bring about a greater percentage increase in distance, if all of the other factors remain constant. For example, a 10 percent increase in speed of release in

Figure 1

Figure 2

shot putting and discus throwing produces an increase of as much as 21 percent in distance.

While the athlete must continually attempt to increase the implement's speed at release (in order to obtain an increase in the distance thrown), he must avoid increasing one velocity component (horizontal or vertical) without also increasing the other. Otherwise, the angle of release is likely to be too high or too low and the distance of the throw will be reduced, even though the release velocity has been increased.

GROUND REACTION

The forces that can be applied to the implement—both vertical and horizontal—require resistance from firm ground; as the athlete thrusts against the implement, he receives a counter-thrust from the ground beneath him. This is called ground reaction and is an important part of Newton's third law of motion, "To every action there is an equal and opposite reaction; or the mutual actions of two bodies in contact are always equal and opposite in direction." Without the resistance from the ground, the powerful actions of the thrower would bring about equal and opposite reactions within his body and the implement would not travel very far.

A 160-pound (73 kg.) person sitting on the ground exerts 160 pounds of force against the ground and the ground pushes back with 160 pounds of force. However, if the 160-pound person decided to jump to his feet, he would have to push against the ground with a force greater than his body weight and the ground would "react" with an equal force, allowing him to lift his body into an erect position.

If the 160-pounder in a standing position suddenly pushed against the ground with a force of 260 pounds (118 kg.), the ground would push back with an equal force of 260 pounds and the person would have 100 pounds (45 kg.) of lift—either to lift himself off the ground (as in the jumping events) or to help him lift something away from the ground (as in the throwing events).

From this, two important points become apparent: (1) The forces that contribute to the acceleration of a throwing implement can be initiated much more effectively while the thrower is in contact with the ground, but not nearly so effectively while he is in the air. (2) The greater the forces applied against the ground, the greater the results in forces against the implement.

ANGLE OF RELEASE

No matter which of the throwing events is being considered, there is a particular optimum throwing angle for every attempt, no matter what ability the individual thrower happens to possess. However, it is not necessarily the same angle for each thrower in an event, or even the same angle for an individual athlete's different attempts in the same competition.

The optimum angle for the projection of a missile is 45 degrees—if the point of landing is at the same level as the height of release. However, since all of the throwing implements are released above ground level, the optimum angle of release must necessarily be less than 45 degrees. How much less depends upon the height of release, the speed of release and, in discus and javelin throwing, on the aerodynamic properties of the implement.

In the shot put, the optimum release angle is between 40 and 42 degrees for good throwers. The angle can be plotted by bisecting the angle formed by a line drawn from the shot at release to the eventual landing point, and a vertical line drawn through the shot at release (Figure 3). Obviously, the greater the velocity of the shot at release, the higher the release angle must be.

Distance of Put in Feet	Optimum Release Angle
25	37° 10'
30	38° 25'
35	39° 20'
40	40° 00'
45	40° 35'
50	41° 00'
55	41° 25'
60	41° 40'
65	41° 55'
70	42° 10'
75	42° 20'

Figure 3—Optimum Release Angles

Because of the effects of air resistance, the opposite is true in discus and javelin throwing. The greater the speed of release, the lower the optimum angle of release. Optimum angles range from 35 to 40 degrees in the discus throw and javelin throw.

In the hammer throw, because the hammer nearly touches the ground on its way to being released, the optimum release angle is only slightly below 45 degrees, no matter what the hammer thrower's ability.

A thrower who wants to raise his angle of release must do so by increasing the vertical velocity of the implement before releasing it. (He could also do it by decreasing the horizontal velocity, but the implement would not go as far.) A shot putter who wants to raise his angle of release during the arm strike, for example, is unable to make an appreciable change; his speed across the circle coupled with his speed of "lifting" the shot has already effectively determined the angle of release before his arm has a chance to make a contribution.

FLIGHT CURVES

Shots and hammers describe nearly perfect parabolic curves as they travel through the air; disci and javelins describe aerodynamic curves that would be parabolic were it not for the lift and drag effects of air resistance.

Parabolic curves. The moment a shot or hammer is released and is free in the air, the entire flight path of its center of gravity is determined. The speed and angle of the release and the force of gravity after the release cause the implement to follow a perfectly regular curve called a parabola, or parabolic curve.

As was mentioned earlier, release angles are determined by the combination of horizontal and vertical velocities. Once the implement is air-borne, the horizontal component is unaffected by outside forces (except some air resistance), but gravity gradually slows the vertical component to zero and then reverses the process, causing the implement to travel progressively faster and faster as it falls. The result is a parabolic curve. The length of the curve (the distance over the ground from release to landing) is determined by the horizontal component; the height of the curve is determined by the vertical component.

Aerodynamic curves. Because of the design of disci and javelins, air resistance causes them to follow flight curves that are not parabolic. As a discus or javelin sails through the air, the air flowing over the implement moves faster than the air flowing underneath, air pressure is diminished above the implement, and a lifting force is created which helps the implement to sail a greater distance than would have been possible without the aerodynamic design.

For the first portion of discus flight, the angle formed between the plane of the implement and the direction of the relative wind (the angle of attack) is a negative angle and there is no lift. This changes as gravity begins to slow the discus. The last half of the discus flight is marked by a positive angle of attack, and the discus experiences a pronounced lifting.

The javelin's angle of attack is positive throughout most of its flight. Even while descending point first, the javelin is inclined at an angle to the relative wind and is continuing to gain distance as it glides toward earth.

THE IMPLEMENTS

Not only is it important for an athlete to attempt to learn the most advantageous throwing technique and to follow the most beneficial training program, it is also important for him to select the throwing implement that will provide the greatest possible distance.

Shots. Not much can be said about shots, or about the advantage one shot might have over another. The rules determine the weight and shape; only the size may vary.

There is a slight advantage in selecting a shot that is smaller in size. The international rules allow the 16-pound (7.3 kg.) shot to be as small as 4⅜ inches (11.1 cm.) in diameter, ¾ inch (0.2 cm.) smaller than the maximum allowed. NCAA rules allow it to be even smaller—4-7/64 inches (10.4 cm.). U.S. high school rules allow the 12-pound (5.4 kg.) shot to be as small as 3⅞ inches (9.8 cm.) in diameter, also ¾ inch smaller than the maximum size allowed.

Because it encounters less air resistance in flight, the smaller shot will travel slightly farther than the larger shot with the same effort. Recent research shows that a 62-foot (18.9 m.) effort with a 16-pound shot that is 4⅜ inches in diameter will travel 2⅜ inches (6.0 cm.) farther than one that is 5⅛ inches (13.0 cm.) in diameter. This is not a great difference, of course, but keep in mind that the difference between the gold and silver medals in the 1972 Olympic Games was less than ½ inch (1 cm.)!

Surprisingly, there is also a slight aerodynamic advantage in selecting a shot with a rough surface. As the shot travels through the air, a low-pressure pocket forms behind the shot, creating drag and reducing velocity somewhat. Because of the effect the type of surface has on the air passing nearest the shot, the size of the low-pressure pocket behind the shot is reduced when a "rough" shot is used. Thus, drag is reduced and the shot travels farther. The difference is approximately 4¾ inches (12.1 cm.) in a 62-foot effort.

Disci. The exact size, shape and weight of a discus is determined by the rule books, but the distribution of weight within the discus is not. Because of differences in the distribution of weight (which cannot be detected by calipers or scales), some disci can be thrown farther than others, even though released in exactly the same way.

Every discus has a certain moment of inertia, which is determined by the distribution of mass within the discus. If a great amount of mass is concentrated in the center of the discus, it has a low moment of inertia; if most of the mass is distributed around its outer edge, it has a high moment of inertia.

When a discus is thrown, the thrower applies both translational and rotational kinetic energy to the discus—translational energy for the distance and rotational energy for the stabilizing spin. Because a hollow discus with the weight distributed to the outside has a higher moment of inertia than a "solid" discus, its spin continues for a longer time while in the air, allowing it to stay level, gyroscopically. Since the hollow discus continues to spin in the air and does not "peel off" so soon, it sails farther before landing.

While there are obvious advantages in selecting a hollow discus for competition, there are equal disadvantages in selecting a molded rubber or plastic discus. Rubber or plastic disci may be less expensive, and they may be easier to grip than the metal-rimmed, wooden ones, but they won't travel nearly as far. The lead pellets that are molded into rubber and plastic disci settle to the center, which can provide nothing but disadvantage for competition. Molded disci have low moments of inertia, they cannot spin as well in the air, they peel off very rapidly, and they don't go as far.

Javelins. Javelins are aerodynamic implements designed to sail maximum distances according to the abilities of the particular throwers. As a thrower's ability increases, he must begin selecting javelins designed to stay in the air longer.

The aerodynamic principles governing javelin flight are very complicated and are not completely understood. However, it is easy to understand one of the aerodynamic factors contributing to the forward rotation of the javelin in the air—the relationship of the javelin's surface area to its center of gravity.

Since javelins are released in a point-up position but must rotate into a point-down position before landing, the tail section (everything behind the javelin's center of gravity) must have a greater total surface area than the front section. The tail section "catches" the air and the javelin slowly tilts forward. Because it is traveling through the air point-first, wind resistance is minimal as the javelin leaves the thrower's hand. But as the javelin begins to slow and more air catches its tail section, the javelin rotates forward around its center of gravity.

The greater the distance thrown, the slower the forward rotation in the air must be. Obviously, the javelin that is going to be thrown 250 feet (76.2 m.) must be designed so that it turns over in the air more slowly than the javelin that will be thrown only 150 feet (45.7 m.). Thus, the amount of surface area on the tail of the javelin (the part that catches the air) must be proportionately less if the javelin thrower's ability is greater, in order to get the longest possible throw.

This is where javelin design and javelin selection become important. The thrower must select the javelin that will turn over just enough during the time it is in the air so that it lands almost flat, but with the point hitting first.

Hammers. The maximum and minimum dimensions for hammers, as designated in the rule books, allow for two different ways to gain valuable distance.

The formula for determining release velocity in hammer throwing is v=wr (Release Velocity = Turning Speed x Effective Radius of Turning). Thus, even if the thrower does not increase his turning speed, his release velocity will be increased if he is able to increase the effective radius of turning. At a turning speed of 2 revolutions per second, an increase of 1½ inches (3.8 cm.) in effective radius is worth approximately 7 feet (2.13 m.) of increased distance in the throw. At 2.3 revolutions per second, the increase is close to 10 feet (3.0 m.).

International rules allow the hammer's maximum overall distance from the bottom surface of the head to the uppermost surface of the grip to be 3 feet 11¾ inches (121.5 cm.)—1½ inches (3.8 cm.) longer than the minimum length allowed. NCAA rules allow the distance to be even longer—4 feet 1/64 inches (122.0 cm.) or 1 19/32 inches (4.0 cm.) longer than the minimum.

The size of the head may be as small as 4 inches (10.2 cm.) in diameter by international rules, ¾ inches smaller than the maximum allowed. Also, the rules allow the head's center of gravity to be ¼ inch off-center, away from the handle. Therefore, the distance from the handle to the head's center of gravity may be as much as 3 feet 10 inches (117.9 cm.) (with maximum length, minimum head size, and the head's center of gravity off-center by ¼ inch), or as little as 3 feet 7⅞ inches (111.4 cm.)

To insure maximum performance by providing the longest possible effective radius of turning, it is obvious that the thrower should select the hammer with the greatest possible distance between the handle and the head's center of gravity.

24

THE SHOT PUT

Athlete: **Wladyslaw Komar,** *Poland*

Olympic Competition:

Shot Put	1964	9th	59 feet 8½ inches (18.20m.)
Shot Put	1968	6th	63 feet 3 inches (19.28m.)
Shot Put	1972	1st	69 feet 6 inches (21.18m.)

Author: **Julian Koszewski** is Poland's Head Coach of the throwing events. Among the outstanding athletes he has coached are Edmund Piatkowski, former world-record holder in the discus throw, and the 1972 Olympic shot put champion, Wladyslaw Komar.

Figure 1 The putter is preparing himself for the glide. The weight of the body is over the right leg with the right foot placed along the diameter of the circle. The toes of the right foot are placed near the back rim of the circle. Left leg with bent knee is touching the ground with its tiptoes. The trunk is upright. The right shoulder is slightly lower than the left shoulder. The left arm is raised up aslant.

Figures 2-3 The thrower is bending his trunk forward and simultaneously raising his left leg up. His left arm is hanging down. The trunk was too violently bent down and the shot putter is losing his balance. This is forcing him to lean once again on the left leg (Figure 4) and to commence glide action from the beginning (Figure 5).

Figures 6-7 The thrower is approaching his left leg to the right one and thus is gaining a favorable starting position from which to execute the actions with his left leg.

Figure 1   **Figure 2**   **Figure 3**   **Figure 4**

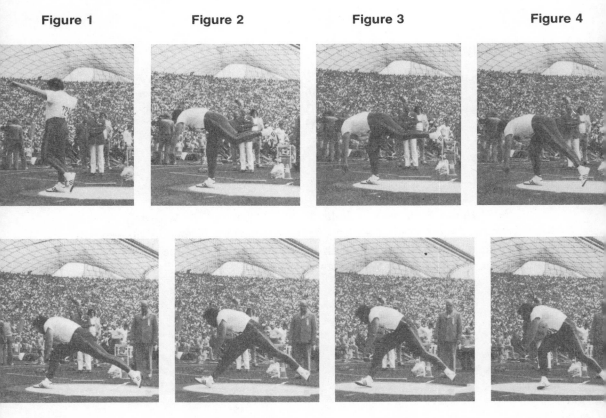

Figure 9   **Figure 10**   **Figure 11**   **Figure 12**

Figures 8-14 The swing of the left leg (Figures 8-10) puts greater pressure on the right leg and thus allows him to make better use of his leg strength, and also increases his horizontal velocity. On the other hand, a left leg motion which follows the shortest path will allow quickest contact with the ground in the throwing position (Figures 8-14). The right leg, which has the task of assuring that the body of the putter has the greatest velocity possible, ends its work in the glide stage with the full straightening of the knee angle (Figure 10). During the flight stage the putter is trying to bring his right foot to the landing position as soon as possible (Figures 12-13). During this time, the left leg begins to bend at the knee and to pass to the left of the diameter of the circle (Figure 14).

Figures 15-17 The incorrect left leg work caused the delay in gaining the double-support throwing position. This mistake also caused the trunk to straighten too early (Figure 15)—the trunk moved forward due "to the force of inertia"—and this, in turn, diminished the effectiveness

Figure 5   **Figure 6**   **Figure 7**   **Figure 8**

Figure 13   **Figure 14**   **Figure 15**   **Figure 16**

of the right leg work (Figures 15-17). The good work of the left arm (Figures 15-17), which does not allow a too early swing of the trunk in the throw direction, reduces the undesirable effects of the incorrect action of the left leg.

Figures 18-20 The putter introduces the right arm into the action. The right shoulder is still lower than the left one (Figure 18) but in the course of straightening it raises up (Figures 19-20). Simultaneously the left leg is straightening at the knee. The preceding error in the left leg action causes the slight deflection of the trunk to the left. This also has an undesirable effect upon the final result of the put.

Figures 21-23 The last stage of the put. The shot putter is trying not to fall away from the circle by springing onto his right leg.

In view of the above, it is worth emphasizing that if the thrower had put his left leg in the throwing position more correctly and maintained the correctness of the other actions, the final result would have been far better.

Figure 17   **Figure 18**   **Figure 19**   **Figure 20**

Figure 21   **Figure 22**   **Figure 23**

25

THE DISCUS THROW

Athlete: **Ludvik Danek,** *Czechoslovakia*

Olympic Competition:

Discus Throw 1964	2nd	198 feet 6½ inches (60.61m.)
Discus Throw 1968	3rd	206 feet 5 inches (62.91m.)
Discus Throw 1972	1st	211 feet 3½ inches (64.40m.)

Author: **Klement Kerssenbrock** is a Professor of Physical Education in Prague, Czechoslovakia, and is a world authority on jumping and throwing techniques. A former pole vaulter, he has been coach of the Czechoslovakian women's team at the Olympic Games (1948), and national coach of the Yugoslavian team. A prolific writer, he has authored 13 texts and numerous magazine articles on track and field.

Figure 1   **Figure 2**   **Figure 3**   **Figure 4**

The discus thrower influences the discus partly in turning his own body, and partly in traveling across the circle. At the climax of the throw he increases the speed with an upward body-thrust and a swing of his right arm (Figure 19).

In the first double-support phase (Figures 1-5) it is possible to influence the discus mainly by turning. One leads the discus with the arm extended far from the body to obtain a large radius.

In the following first single-support phase (Figures 5-10) it is not possible to accelerate the turn. The turn continues only by inertia. On the other hand, the discus can be effectively influenced in traveling across the

Figure 9   **Figure 10**   **Figure 11**   **Figure 12**

Figure 5   **Figure 6**   **Figure 7**   **Figure 8**

circle. Here the thrower draws the discus with the extended arm behind his back.

   In the flight phase (Figures 10-11) the discus cannot be actively influenced, so it is necessary to come early into an advantageous support phase. Therefore, the extended arm is trailed with the discus near to the body. The radius of turn gets shorter and the angular velocity increases.

   In the second single-support phase (Figures 11-14) it is again impossible to accelerate the turn. Therefore the thrower applies a so-called pseudo-rotation. While his shoulder, his right arm and the discus lag behind (note the discus in relation with the background in Figures 12-13),

Figure 13   **Figure 14**   **Figure 15**   **Figure 16**

Figure 17   **Figure 18**

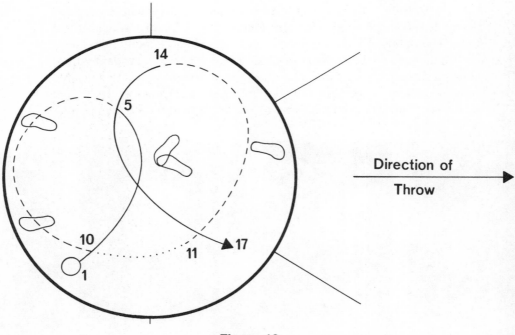

Direction of
Throw

Figure 19

he turns his hips and legs. So not only does he come early into the advantageous double-support phase (Figures 14-17), but his body also acquires great muscle tension, which is important for the final effort.

In the second double-support phase the discus is influenced by turning, by progress across the circle, and by the action of the arm swing.

Let us observe how Ludvik Danek meets these various requirements. Danek does a one-and-three-quarters turn, in which the discus describes a path of about 29 feet 6½ inches (9m.)—Figure 19.

First double-support phase	4 feet 11 inches	(1.5m.)
First single-support phase	8 feet 2½ inches	(2.5m.)
Flight phase	1 foot 7¾ inches	(0.5m.)
Second single-support phase	6 feet 6¾ inches	(2.0m.)
Second double-support phase	8 feet 2½ inches	(2.5m.)
	29 feet 6½ inches	(9.0m.)

Figure 1 Danek uses only one preliminary swing, though the majority of throwers use two. However, for Danek's full concentration and relaxation it is sufficient. It is in keeping with his nature. His legs are nearly stretched, he turns the body and the arm with the discus to the right as far as possible, and from there he begins to pivot.

Figures 2-5 Danek starts very slowly. Both legs are bent; the body-weight has been shifted from the right to the left leg; both feet are on the ball. The left foot and the left knee are leading. The right foot lags in contact with the ground to support the turn. The hips thus outrun the shoulders.

Figures 6-10 As soon as his right toe loses ground contact, Danek leads the right knee quickly forward and starts to take-off across the circle from the left leg. This phase is similar to a starting step. In this throw Danek takes off too high instead of forward. Therefore his progress across the circle is insufficient. It seems that Danek did not want to take any risks with this throw.

Figure 11 The thrower is without ground contact for a short moment. Owing to his preceding faults the discus is far from the body. The radius stays long instead of short.

Figures 12-14 Danek lands on his right foot but, owing to his high flight phase, his right leg is not bent enough. His initial position for the final action is too high. First he must go down (compare Figures 11, 12 and 13) and this is wasteful of energy. Danek therefore tries to plant his left foot as fast as possible in order to gain an advantageous position for the final action. Thus the important body twist develops.

Figures 14-17 The left foot is landing, but too far to the right, so that the throwing position is too close and does not permit a sufficient range for the shifting of the body weight from the right to the left leg. This also indicates that Danek threw very cautiously in this attempt. As soon as Danek's left foot is grounded, he turns his toes and with them his legs and his hips in the throwing direction. The right leg pushes the body farther forward. The left leg lifts him, but unfortunately not enough—this is an old fault of Danek's. In the final effort Danek's shoulders catch his hips and the arm with the discus comes up with terrific speed. The left arm keeps balance during the throw and does not apply any effort backwards. At the finish Danek has both feet in contact with the ground.

Figure 18 After the throw Danek does a reverse. With a full-effort throw Danek comes near to the circle with his right foot. Certainly there was not enough power in this toss.

26

THE JAVELIN THROW

Athlete: **Ruth Fuchs,** *East Germany*

Olympic Competition:
Javelin Throw 1972   1st   209 feet 7 inches (63.88m.)
                                          (Olympic Record)

Author: **Gustaf Laurell** has been Chief National Coach in Sweden since 1971. A former National Coach in both Finland (1948-1958) and Sweden (1958-1970), he has also served as coach of the European team vs. the Americas (1967) and has lectured at numerous international track and field clinics.

In my opinion this is probably not one of Ruth Fuchs' best throws. In fact, I would rather suggest that it is technically a rather poor one. The main fault is that she is not using the power coming from checking the forward momentum by using the left leg.

In step 1 (Figures 1-4) she starts withdrawing the javelin using the common over-the-shoulder method; the step is high and powerful, and the purpose is to prepare for the ''going down.'' Step 2 (Figures 5-6) is very

Figure 1   **Figure 2**   **Figure 3**

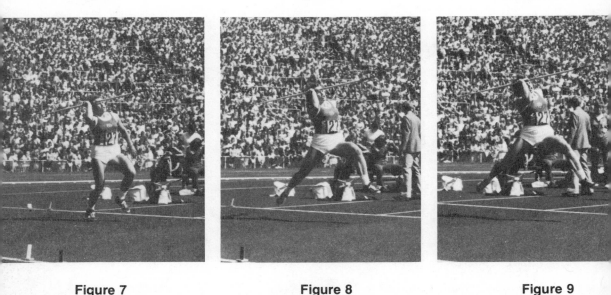

Figure 7   **Figure 8**   **Figure 9**

short. The implement is in the final position for the throw in Figure 8. In the same picture Fuchs makes an attempt to increase the backward lean by stretching the right leg as she goes into step 3. Step 4, the penultimate stride, is rather short. It should be longer in order to get even more backward lean and to make it possible to make a shift of the legs in the air, so that the left leg is in front of the right leg when the right foot lands. By using this method, the thrower can get a long last stride and, at the same time, a fast left-leg contact with the ground. In Figure 12, Fuchs

Figure 4 **Figure 5** **Figure 6**

Figure 10 **Figure 11** **Figure 12**

lands with the right foot too much in front of the body which means that she is losing speed. This is reflected in the very short last stride (the throwing position). If the last step were long enough, the right foot would be dragged on the ground before the left foot was grounded. In Figure 16 the left leg is bent too much and will be straightened too late—when the center of gravity has already passed the supporting left foot. She therefore does not get a powerful arched position of the body. There is, of course, an arch but only a weak one. The distance and time that she now has left is too short for a really powerful throw.

Figure 13   **Figure 14**

Figure 17   **Figure 18**

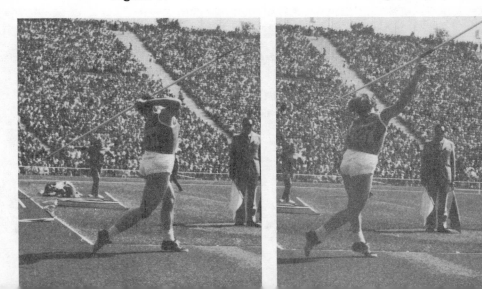

Compared to the throws of Lusis, Wolfermann, and Kinnunen, for example, Fuchs is not able to get a good stopping action from the left leg. Checking the forward momentum by having a long last step will cause an acceleration to that part of the body above the center of gravity of the torso. This acceleration also occurs about the longitudinal axis of the body—the speed of the right side of the body will also increase. Fuchs' handling of the javelin is perfect and the direction of the throw will be along its line. There is no "wobbling" at all when the implement is leaving her hand.

Figure 15

Figure 16

Figure 19

Figure 20

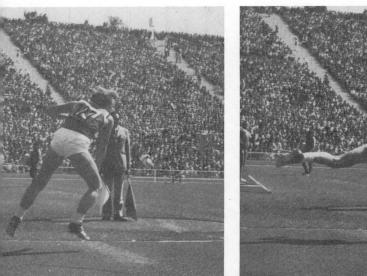

27

THE HAMMER THROW

Athlete: **Anatoliy Bondarchuk,** *U.S.S.R.*

Olympic Competition:
    Hammer Throw 1972   1st   247 feet 8½ inches (75.5m.)
                                           (Olympic Record)

    Author: **Gabor Simonyi** is Director of Physical Education in North Battleford Comprehensive High School, Saskatchewan, Canada. A former Hungarian champion in the long jump, triple jump and 200m. hurdles, he coached in Hungary (1954-1963), Iceland (1963-1964), and England (1964-1966) before moving to Canada, where he is presently a national coach. He has served as coach of the Icelandic team at the European Championships (1958, 1962) and the Olympic Games (1960) and as coach of the Canadian team at the Commonwealth Games (1970) and Pan-American Games (1971). Widely regarded as a leading international authority on the hammer throw, he is co-author (with Sam Felton) of *Modern Hammer Technique*, has coached such well-known hammer throwers as Gyula Zsivotsky and Sandor Eckshmidt, and has worked with many of the United States' leading throwers.

In hammer throwing two masses rotate about a tilted (and, of course, invisible) common axis: (1) the thrower's body and (2) the ball (hammer-head). During the turns the athlete moves this common axis from the rear to the front of the circle by a specific footwork.

Two forces, working in opposite directions and counter-balancing each other, are at work during the turns: (1) centripetal (pulling-in, by the thrower), and (2) centrifugal (pulling-out, by the hammer-head). As the hammer's velocity increases, the thrower must increase the centripetal force. For example, if the hammer's velocity doubles, the centripetal force must be increased four times. (The force of gravity plus the centripetal force exerted by the athlete is proportional to the square of the hammer's linear velocity.)

Figure 1   **Figure 2**   **Figure 3**

Since the velocity of the hammer increases after each turn, the maintenance of balance and control is progressively more difficult. Due to the increasing centrifugal force there is a strong tendency to be rotated forward. To avoid this, the athlete has to "sit-in" ever deeper thereby improving his stability.

The thrower accelerates his hammer by using both horizontal and vertical components of force. Through friction between his feet and the surface he applies force horizontally by moving the tilted common axis across the circle thus imparting centripetal force. He can do this only by maintaining his body weight over his pivoting foot throughout the turns and the throw.

A body torque (hips and legs lead the hammer-head through a trunk twist) also contributes to the further acceleration of the hammer. Whenever the hammer is not at 90 degrees to the curve along which it is moving, it will be accelerating.

Further acceleration is resulting from the hammer's moving up and down during the turns from high to low point. This acceleration is especially effective when the hammer is "falling" down to its low point. Working with gravity to increase the velocity of the down-falling hammer, the thrower sits down just before it drops to its low point. The gradual steepening of the plane of the hammer also imparts vertical speed to the hammer.

Figure 4   **Figure 5**   **Figure 6**

To stay in balance and control, the thrower must accelerate his hammer gradually (not suddenly) making proper body reactions possible.

Last but not least, the great importance of the longest possible radius must not be overlooked: the longer this effective radius the more peripheral velocity for the hammer-head results. Hence the importance of allowing shoulders and arms to be pulled out by the hammer without, however, permitting the hammer to bend the upper body forward during the faster turns (second and third).

Obviously, everything a hammerthrower does in the circle after he has started his action must in some way (directly and/or indirectly) contribute to the gradual but powerful accelerating of the hammer so that it might be delivered at the end with the greatest velocity possible.

In the sequence, Figures 1-11 show the first preliminary wind, 12-15 the second; 15-16 show the transition (from high point to low) from the winds to the first turn; 16-21, the first turn; 22-25, the second; 26-31, the third and, in this case, the last turn. Figures 32-35 show the delivery and Figures 36-37, the recovery (reverse).

Most hammerthrowers use one of two methods to start their preliminary winding: (1) the hammer-head is lying on the surface in varying positions behind the thrower, on his right side. From this stationary position, reaching back for the grip by twisting his shoulders right and placing his bodyweight on his right foot, the athlete pulls the hammer up,

Figure 7   **Figure 8**   **Figure 9**

forward and to the left. (2) the hammer-head is lying on the thrower's left side in the circle (and behind his left heel or off it) with his left hand in the grip. From here he swings the hammer up, forward and to the right side where his right hand joins the left hand in the grip. Bondarchuk is using this second method. Users of this swinging method claim that they can set up a rhythm which helps them in the correct execution of the winds.

The first of the preliminary winds merely serves as a rehearsal for the more important second one and therefore it is slower and more casual in its execution. Although only a rehearsal, the first wind serves also for the establishment of the plane of the hammer as well as the location of the low point. When we examine Figures 4 and 5 (first wind), and compare them with Figure 11 (same phase during the second wind), we can see that in 4 and 5 the elbows are well bent (a sign of casualness), whereas in Figure 11 they are straight.

The throw we analyze is a long one: 75.50m. (247 feet plus). Although Bondarchuk's technique is very good, it nevertheless is not entirely flawless. (Even the best throwers, including Olympic champions, do make mistakes.) Bondarchuk's consistently high performances are the result of good technique, great strength, a heavy but explosive body, and diligence, to mention the most important ingredients only.

Figure 1 (Initial stance—feet apart, a little more than shoulder width for stability—beginning of preliminary winds.)

Using the less common of the two starting methods, Bondarchuck

Figure 10   **Figure 11**   **Figure 12**

has swung his hammer from the left side by his left hand, now to swing it back on his right where he places his right hand on top of his left.

The direction of the first swinging movement from the left has an influence on the location of the low point in the ensuing winds. If the direction is too much to the right (across and in front of the body), the low point is more likely to be situated too far on the athlete's right side (a disadvantage). On the other hand, if the initial direction is straight forward or a little to the left, the low point will fall more in front of the thrower (as it should).

Figure 2 The hammer, after the initial swing, has now swung to the right side, and it is now time to put the right hand on top of the left one in the grip.

Bodyweight is on the right foot and, due to the present location of the hammer, the shoulders have twisted to the right.

The head remaining in its original position controls the degree of shoulder rotation and is the key to proper orientation.

General body position: erect.

Figure 3 The real winding is now beginning: the shoulders have started unwinding leftward and the forward pull of the hammer is under way.

To achieve firm balance, Bondarchuk inclines his trunk slightly forward keeping his head in plumb-line with his right foot.

Figure 13   **Figure 14**   **Figure 15**

Figure 4 Body weight is now halfway through shifting from right toward the left foot.

Since the first wind is a little less important than the second, as mentioned before, Bondarchuk does execute the first part rather casually.

A slight bending of the knees here contributes to stability.

Figure 5 Bodyweight now having shifted leftward, and the hammer-head having almost reached its low point in front of the right foot, the most difficult part of the winding is about to begin: leading the hammer-head smoothly around the body in a big circle and in the proper plane (as "flat" as possible).

Head must remain still to provide firmness and orientation.

Figure 6 Bondarchuk has shifted his bodyweight as far leftward as it will be during the winds. He has already started the preparation for the proper "leading" of the hammerhead around; he has bent his right elbow and lifted it while keeping his left one low.

Figure 7 Simultaneously pushing his hips back to the right to counterbalance the hammer's momentary leftward pull, his body assumes a sideways bend as his right arm continues to rise while he still keeps his left elbow in a low position. He is shifting his weight to the right.

Figure 8 With much of the bodyweight now back on the right foot, as the hammer is approaching its high point behind him, Bondarchuk has lifted both elbows high (it would have been better to keep the left elbow

Figure 16   **Figure 17**   **Figure 18**

low) on the right side of the head. His shoulders are well on the way to the right having twisted from their previous position (Figures 6 and 7).

Figure 9 This is the most difficult and inconvenient phase of winding. After the hammer has reached its high point behind the body, the thrower, having twisted his shoulders to the right, is now trying to establish contact with the downcoming implement by reaching back to the right with his arms as far as he can.

Bondarchuk, at this particular phase, has his left shoulder too high. As a result, he is in a rather awkward position. Had he maintained the slight bending over of his trunk ("overhand"), he could have kept his left shoulder a lot lower and thereby avoided the unnecessary strain.

Figure 10 Bondarchuk has reached back to the right to get the hammer down smoothly—straighten arms and let the shoulders out well before the hammer reaches its low point.

Figure 11 As the body weight is·moving toward the left leg, the hammer is running through its low point. The head is still maintaining its position: "looking" slightly to the right. Arms now have straightened, shoulders are "out." The pull of the hammer is mainly counterbalanced by the hips.

Figures 9-11 demonstrate the rehearsal for the so-called transition phase which is nothing else but the phase lasting from the high point to

Figure 19   **Figure 20**   **Figure 21-**

the low point and includes the early contact, the settling (bending of knees), and the transfer of body weight from the right toward the left leg.

Figures 12-14 In the second wind Bondarchuk increases the speed of his movement and, as a result, the velocity of the hammer-head. After a relatively slow and somewhat casual first wind he is in earnest now to get ready for his turns.

With regard to the ensuing turns and the final throw, in relation to the thrower's body and the direction of his initial stand plus the direction (line) of his turns in the circle, the location of the low and high points during the successive turns is extremely important. A straight line running from the low point to the high point should be in line with the direction of the turns and the throw. Thus, the low points should be roughly in front of the thrower while, correspondingly, the high point should be behind him. However, since the low point has a tendency to move gradually leftward during the turns, it should be just off the right foot (to the right) during the winds. When it comes to the delivery, it (the low point) will have moved sufficiently leftward, but not past the left foot.

If the low point is located too far on the thrower's right during winding, the high point, correspondingly, will be situated on the opposite (left) side. Suppose the low point ''hits'' at 270 degrees on the right during the winds. As a result, the high point will be somewhere at 90 degrees direction (on the left).

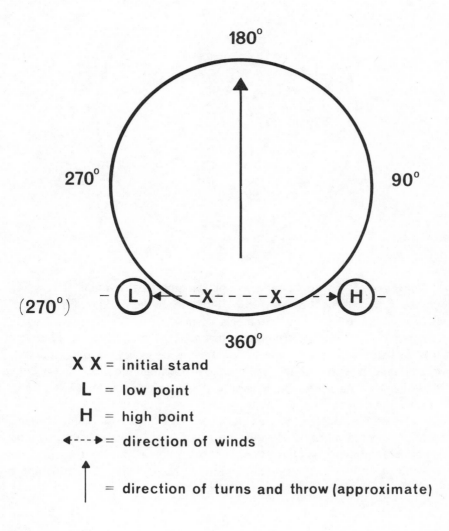

X X = initial stand

L = low point

H = high point

◄---► = direction of winds

= direction of turns and throw (approximate)

This set-up of the low and high points does not coincide with the direction of the turns and the throw (180 degrees). For this reason it is likely to result in trailing; too steep a plane for the hammer; deviating from the proper line of turns; losing power in the delivery; and a throw far out to the left (even outside of the throwing sector). Not only trailing but also an upper body counter might result from such a set-up.

However, when the low and high points lie more in line with the direction of the turns and the throw, the preceding faults can easily be avoided.

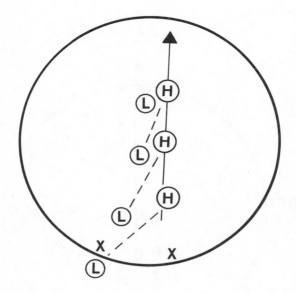

Figure 15 As the hammer is approaching its low point, a very important action of the thrower occurs right here in the middle of transition. Bondarchuk, to keep the hammer's plane "flat" (low) as well as to achieve the longest radius possible, has not only bent his knees, but also bent forward in the waist. This action puts his hips back to counterbalance the hammer's pull. At the same time it permits him to "chase" the hammer-head far out to the longest distance possible from his center of gravity.

Figure 16 Before the hammer-head "hits" its low point, Bondarchuk, to secure an early "lead" (hips and legs to go in front of upper body and hammer), has already started his footwork for the first turn. As a result, his hip-line is not parallel with his shoulder-line. Since his upper body remains "facing" the hammer head, this is not trailing, only a hip-lead over shoulders (body torque).

Figure 17 Countering the hammer's pull only by the hips and legs, Bondarchuk's upper body remains basically straight with only a slight inclination (in the waist) toward the hammer-head. This slight forward bend in this direction is permissible here where the pull from the hammer-head is still small—this being only the beginning of the first turn with relatively low velocity. (During the same phase in the second turn—Figure 23—no such inclination is present anymore for then the pull is a lot greater.)

In Figure 16 we can see Bondarchuk's head starting to turn leftward.

Figure 22   **Figure 23**   **Figure 24**

An advanced thrower can do this without allowing his shoulders to also turn left thus losing the "lead." For beginners and novices, however, it might be better to keep the head more in the direction of the hammer-head at this phase. Bondarchuk does a good job of moving his head and hips together while leaving shoulders, upper body (and, of course, the hammer) behind; however, he too makes the mistake during his last turn of turning his head too far ahead, an action that shortens his radius.

Figure 18 Having delayed his right foot on the surface during the first part of his turn (the two-feet-on-the-ground phase) for good balance and rhythm, Bondarchuk, while continuing his turn on the outer edge of his pivot (left) foot's heel, is now breaking contact with the surface.

Allowing the hammer to "pull out" his shoulders and thereby causing it to run on the widest orbit possible (long radius), he counters the
hammer's pull with his hips and legs leaning away while keeping his
upper body basically upright. (A forward bend at this phase could pull
him forward. The consequence would be a heavy landing on the right foot
at the completion of the turn.)

Figure 19 Correctly, Bondarchuk is "carrying" his right leg close
and low to the pivoting left one. To facilitate an early landing and the
keeping of his lower body lead, such a "tight" turn is imperative.

The countering of the hammer's pull is achieved by the hips as well
as the bend in the knee of the pivoting leg.

Figure 25   **Figure 26**   **Figure 27**

The hammer is nearly at its high point now and therefore a more
vertical force being present, a "sinking" of the body must be performed
to avoid a lifting of it. (Naturally, since this is the first turn with the speed
still relatively low, this "sitting" down, or "sinking" is a mild one as
yet.)

If a straightening were permitted at this phase in the pivot knee, the
upper body would have to bend forward: balance would be impaired or
lost.

The outer edge roll of the pivot foot now is going on the ball part of
the foot.

The right arm, correctly, is straight—a sign of proper torque—and not only are the arms "behind" the hips but "behind" the whole upper body as well.

Figure 20 To make landing even faster, the right foot "hits" (or alights) on the surface with the toe pointing outward (to the right).

The forward bend of the upper body is deliberate at this moment; Bondarchuk does it to achieve the longest radius possible. Another reason is to enable himself to accelerate the hammer head horizontally a moment later by a centripetal pull.

As soon as the right foot lands, it helps immediately to push and turn the legs and hips ahead of the hammer, thus accelerating it as well as maintaining the "lead."

Figure 28   **Figure 29**   **Figure 30**

During the turn(s) the weight of the body should remain mainly on the pivot foot and even in landing this should be so. A "heavy" landing on the right foot is a proof of improper balance; this in turn then renders the right foot helpless.

Figure 22 A quick "uprighting" of the upper body from its preceding momentary bend-over by a "rocking" back of the body onto the left heel combined with the continued turning left of the feet imparts acceleration to the hammer-head. However, this first real acceleration of the hammer must not be out of proportion—there are two more turns to follow. (Acceleration must be gradually increasing.)

Figures 23-24 These figures represent roughly the same phase as

Figures 17-19, (i.e. they show the second turn). In Figure 24 we may notice the bend in the right elbow. This bend is a consequence of Bondarchuk's eagerness to complete the second turn early; his head turns too far ahead of the shoulders (even in front of the hips). It would be better to keep it more in line with the wire shaft.

Figure 25 Figure 25 shows an excellent lead of legs and hips over shoulders while the vertical component of force is at work to accelerate the hammer-head on its way down from the high point. Bondarchuk does his job here well; he is ''sitting down.'' Notice the toe of the right foot: it points to the right. Figures 26-31 illustrate the last turn.

·   *Figure 26* Without the slightest hesitation, our thrower is going on with his turning with hips and legs way ahead of the hammer.

Figure 31   **Figure 32**   **Figure 33**

The additional acceleration of the hammer has already begun by the quick ''uprighting'' of the upper body, even though the hammer-head has not yet ''hit'' its low point.

·   *Figure 27* The sideways pull continues (due to the great lead). Feet, legs and hips have already turned a near 90 degrees while the hammer is just at its low point. The head is perhaps a little farther left than it should be.

By his fast rotation after landing Bondarchuk not only succeeded in maintaining his ''lead,'' but also managed to increase it. Thereby his acceleration became more pronounced.

Figure 28 Because of too much leading with his head, Bondarchuk at this moment appears to be hauling in his hammer a little. Notice his shoulders: they are far from being "pulled out." Look at his arms, especially the right one; his elbows are slightly bent. This equals a shortening of radius.

The "uprighting" of the upper body (a significant contribution to increased horizontal acceleration of the hammer-head) has just been completed.

Figure 29 Having thus lost some of the proper lead as well as some length of radius (shoulders have somewhat caught up with the hips at this moment), we see Bondarchuk's right elbow still bent. Had he not permitted his head to race ahead and tilt a little before, he might have been able to avoid this mistake.

The hammer's upward velocity is now tremendous. Even though he tries to sit down against this upward pull, it almost lifts him off the surface.

A clear indication of the centrifugal force's magnitude at this moment is the height of the right knee and the gap (sideways) between the two knees. During the very fast last turn with a fantastic pull from the hammer it is extremely difficult to keep the right knee (and leg in general) close to the left one. However, every effort must be made to have the "tightest" turn possible.

Notice the high point here and compare it to Figure 19 (first turn) and Figure 24 (second turn) to realize that in each succeeding turn the high point rises progressively, an indication of the increased vertical component of the acceleration forces.

If we compare Figure 19 to Figure 29, it is at once obvious to us that while in Figure 19 the lower body (hips and legs) does the countering action (correctly), in Figure 29 we can see a slight upper body countering (incorrect). A vertical line would connect the left shoulder with the left hip in Figure 19, whereas a similar vertical line in Figure 29 from the shoulder would "miss" the hip.

Figure 30 By "dropping" down (bending knees), so that the left knee is relatively close to the surface, Bondarchuk keeps accelerating the down-racing hammer, at the same time setting up a tremendous lead with the hammer-head way up and behind.

From his previous momentary trailing (Figure 29) he quickly recovered (amazingly well) and is now ready to explode into the delivery as soon as his right foot is down. The early landing of his right foot is facilitated by the deep kneebend in his left knee.

Notice how well he maintains his bodyweight over his left leg and also that now both arms are fairly straight.

Figure 31 Letting the hammer pull his shoulders "out" (thus still maintaining a long radius), Bondarchuk, now that his right foot (on the toe) is on the surface, is starting a powerful and very fast pull leftward while continuing the turn on his feet. The range of this pull is fantastically long.

This sideways pull accelerates the down-racing hammer even more and concentrates his body weight totally on his left leg as well.

Figure 32 The sideways pull is now completed, although the hammer-head is still relatively far from its low point.

Look at his head . . . an indication of the great effort with which Bondarchuk has been pulling sideways (leftward).

Figure 33 With the hammer almost at its low point in front of him,

Figure 34   **Figure 35**

Bondarchuk is now executing a most powerful "uprighting" of the upper body with a lean of the whole body into the direction of the throw. This movement imparts even more velocity to the hammer. To lean back against this fantastic pull requires great leg, lower back and shoulder strength.

As may be seen, Bondarchuk's knees are still slightly bent. The work so far has mainly been executed by the upper body with the legs acting as supporting force.

The backward lean is led by the head (tilted back with the chin high up).

Figure 34 The turning on the feet continues and now the hammer, having already raced through the low point, is on its way up. Now is the time to quickly straighten the left knee while leaning back against the pull even more. The hammer is moving so fast now that it can hardly be seen.

Notice the hips (pelvis) that, in consequence of the backward lean of the upper body, are "under" the lift (i.e., are over the supporting legs) thus receiving the full power from the legs.

Figure 35 Having gone into the turn with the feet almost 90 degrees, the left foot has tilted to its outer edge. (This is as far as the turn goes.)

The arms in the final lift have come up to shoulder height but do not bend. (With the pull so powerful, it would be extremely difficult even to bend them). The backward lean, naturally, is now in the 270 degree direction, and is at its fullest. Notice the arch of the back and the total

Figure 36   **Figure 37**

backward (upward) tilt of the head.

Figure 36 With the hammer now gone, the upper body has already snapped back to the vertical.

Bodyweight is still over the left leg, clear proof of a properly executed delivery (over and from the left leg).

The high, above-the-head position of the arms is a natural reaction.

Figure 37 In the final balancing act Bondarchuk's main concern is to avoid fouling. He is about to reverse; his right foot is already in the air.

After well-executed turns and throw, usually there is no problem in staying inside the circle after delivery. The real reason for a foul is hardly ever found in the delivery.